MW01142052

SENTENCED
BUT NOT
SILENCED

(The Paradigm Of A Poet's Prophecy)

 Walter H. Martin-El

authorHOUSE®

AuthorHouse™ LLC
1663 Liberty Drive
Bloomington, IN 47403
www.authorhouse.com
Phone: 1-800-839-8640

Published by AuthorHouse   08/30/2013

ISBN: 978-1-4817-6579-4 (sc)
ISBN: 978-1-4817-6578-7 (hc)
ISBN: 978-1-4817-6577-0 (e)

Library of Congress Control Number: 2013910985

Any people depicted in stock imagery provided by Thinkstock are models,
and such images are being used for illustrative purposes only.
Certain stock imagery © Thinkstock.

This book is printed on acid-free paper.

Because of the dynamic nature of the Internet, any web addresses or links contained in
this book may have changed since publication and may no longer be valid. The views
expressed in this work are solely those of the author and do not necessarily reflect the
views of the publisher, and the publisher hereby disclaims any responsibility for them.

SUMMARY

This book is a prophetic peek into the heart of this author, through the eyeglass of his mind, reasoning, belief, and faith. The laughter and lamentations expressed herein are blatant examples of how poetry can shed a light of revelation on the unknown, reveal the hidden wisdom of the most darkest of hours lived by the misguided fool, and tell a story a lot better than a painting worth a thousand words.

This is a mental diary-like manuscript compiled of emotions, moods, experiences of the heart, prophetic visions, relationship rules, and ethereal thoughts all fueled by Allah-inspired direction and written to and for those who have only silenced their minds in order to become aware of His presence in them and of the presence of the storms that are forever raging in us and around us.

These are writings and songs of joy, encouragement, and inspiration sometimes painted with warning and other times shaded with the answers to the "why's" that often pester our consciousness and unconsciousness.

Finally, this book is a formal invitation to the reader. It is a request for your company that you might journey with the author outside of the realms of this soul-plane to a Spiritual plane, elevating from this level where man strives to be "man with god" to a level where we here, are ascending to be "God in Man".

TABLE OF CONTENTS

DEDICATION

I would simply like to dedicate this book to EVERYONE who's
been imprisoned physically, emotionally, or psychologically
but had the courage to hang on to your sanity, to your
endurance, to your perseverance, and to your voice that
thunders from the inside outward; adamantly refusing
to never give up, give in, or ever be SILENCED!

ACKNOWLEDGEMENTS

I would love to first and foremost acknowledge, praise, and extend my honors and gratitude to the Great and Merciful Creator of all the worlds and Father of the universe…The One True God ALLAH! Without Him, I am not possible. With Him, I AM THAT I AM!

I would like to pause and say, "Thank You!" to my Team-(help meet) - Mate and Life-Partner, Mrs. Talitha C. Martin. Without Her, I am only half of me. With Her, We are One in everything and Everything in one.

I want to acknowledge all of my beautiful children. I won't name you all here. But know that not one of you is left out of my heart. (Martins, Chiles', Bradfords, Thomas', and Stiffs).

Of course I don't want to hesitate to acknowledge my mother, the Vine of which I have been Allah's fruit produced for the uplifting of all fallen humanity. Albeit, with Allah's Will and allowing, I breathe because of her. She is my Lifeline and Supreme Source; my Connection back to the good earth and great universe. I love You to LIFE!

I would like to acknowledge my friend and dear brother again as I have in other literary projects of mine, James McCloud, aka (J.B.). This is simply because at one time, you were probably the biggest fan and critic of my poetry and story writing. I think I might have recited each one of these pieces to you before they were ever placed in this book or any other book besides my personal, wireless notebook. I always loved and welcomed your feedback, whether it was full of praise or constructive criticism. I love you! Though sentenced, I know you have never been and never will be silenced. May Peace always dwell and abide with thee.

I definitely want to acknowledge my fans and supporters. You all are the greatest. I also want to encourage and inspire you to reach for your visions and don't just settle for the dream. Don't be discouraged or dismayed by the haters.

Last but not least, I would like to acknowledge Authorhouse Publishing And all of your staff who persuaded me to go ahead and just do it. Thank you for the help, hard work, and advice that was applied to aiding and assisting me in completing this project. Thank you for continuously bugging me, e-mailing me, and blowing up my phone to push me into publishing this literary work expeditiously.

I love all of my sisters and brothers. If I left anyone out of these acknowledgements that feel I should have acknowledged them, I apologize and I pray that you charge it to my mind and not my heart.

INTRODUCTION

My pen is still the greatest machine I know. It is still my favorite instrument; the printer to the hard drive in my mind. It is the microphone of which my soul uses to speak to everything and to everyone outside of me. As it glides across the smooth surfaces of these pages, one by one , (every leaf), my every pain; my every rage is expressed; my every joy; when I'm annoyed or filled with happy-ness; when I fell blessed or just overwhelmed and inundated with the gloomy grief that can oft times entomb me and consume me.

My pen is what I love. Because it tells the story of what I love; what I ache and long for more of; what I should do a whole lot less of. It describes what is indescribable in my regular, everyday conversation to regular, everyday people. My pen is the path to my passions, sketching the window panes of my desires; exploding when my patience expires; spreading the flames of my emotional fires turning, churning, and burning in the heavens and the hells of my thoughts.

My pen is who I am...where I lose my self, then find myself, then marvel at how wonderfully new I am. This pen that writes, Sentenced But Not Silenced, which is telling the story of the old me; singing the glory of the coming of the bold me; revealing all life ever showed me and reminding me of all ALLAH ever told me. They couldn't silence me because they never controlled me.

Yesterday, I was just a small measure of who I am today. Today, I'm an even smaller measure of who I was yesterday. Tomorrow is the illusion that hides the truth that this moment is forever

SENTENCED BUT NOT SILENCED
THE PARADIGM OF A POET'S PROPHECY

My country tis of thee; slave land of misery and no liberty…
Let's now tell them what you did to me…
How all those years you kept my kids from me.

How far is it from television to federal super-vision?
What's the average population
In your max-security super-prisons?

You say you fight crime; yours is a system
that looks like crime.
Is that why I'm crying at night-time?
In my six by nine?

Doing hard time for trying to hustle through hard times.
And thanks to you, these nickels and dimes
Wasn't too hard to find.

But did you think you'd Silence me with that sentence
And shut me up?
I didn't give up when the D.A. wouldn't let me up!
And the judge tried to eff me up!

Here's my testimony and I don't need no witness box!
U.S prosecutors push weight around like…
Over zealous fitness jocks.

The correctional officer's gettin' his rocks off;
Laughin' his socks off.

You'll be lookin' for him when the riot pops off;
And he might be found with his whole top chopped off.

Don't tell me to knock it off.
Though I was sentenced, I'm not SILENCED!

Let's talk about how you kicked in my door
And whooped my ass – was that domestic violence?

To break up families, friendships,
And cut the strings to community ties?

Do you think that your vision to see me dead
Is immune to my eyes?

I know exactly where your opportunity lies…
In the middle-East…right on that line
Where the Sheite and Sunni divides.

Who is he who decides to judge the lives
Of ALLAH'S people, Prophets, Angels, and guides?

As sure as the wind glides and the horse strides,
No one will hide when His punishment arrives.

And abides where the inner man strives
Somewhere between silence and violence;
Where I choose neither one.

However, please, don't you be the one…
To make me pick either one!

Because the lesser of these two evils will not allow you
To see the sun!

Question Obama: Why do you choose not to free the dumb?
Don't be silenced, people! Cry out, "We done won!"

And Officer, I see your gun.
But that doesn't mean I'ma turn, tuck my tail,
Flee and run.

You may have judged me and sentenced me.
But you didn't steal my cry!
Even though my thoughts are stilled, still I cry!

And who can be as real as I?
You pulled me over and said I was going too fast.

Throwing rocks at me
And all the while, knowing you're glass.

So it's against the law to do anything…
Unless that "anything", is throwing you cash.

As soon as I'm not, you give the warrant to the cop
To go in my stash.

I was sentenced but NOT SILENCED!
So I'm tellin' it like it is.

For instance, Whippings made me think that
Ellen didn't like her kids.

Like, why do Queens get rid of their real hair…
To show how much they dislike their wigs?

Like, why do fathers get locked up…
And refuse to write their kids?

She loves to follow the dog and his bone.
No matter wherever he digs.

Why has the tree of our Nationality
Been reduced to only twigs?

I'ma talk about it and I'm fo' damn sho'
Gon' be about it!

Awareness? Never catch me without it!
How come when Truth is most evident, we doubt it?

When our thinking is supposed to be most clear, we cloud it.
Do whatever you want to do to me? I won't allow it!

I gained knowledge!
Every one of your plans, plots, and schemes towards me's
Been re-routed.

You sentenced us when the first seed of slavery was sprouted.
But now it's over! We have not been SILENCED!
Listen to us shout it.

BELIEVE

You have to believe in who you are. God knows I do!
I believe in me and I believe in you too.

You have to believe in who you are and what you can do.
NEVER give up! Faith will carry you through.

Believe in what's inside.
Don't study the things that others say.

Remember…after every bad night,
Comes sunlight with the day.

Don't stop praying and hoping to achieve.
You can surely conquer all that appears impossible…
If you only believe!

Author's note:
Believing in one's self is essential as well as critical concerning the state of one's own position in the universe of evolution.
First, believe in God. Then believe in "GOD-in Self". Afterwards, believe in self with a confidence and surety that makes others believe in you and all that you believe in, irresistibly.

HOW'D YOU DO IT?

God! – Was I the worst or what?
Sharp pain in your side that would burst a gut.
I had to be cursed for luck.
Born in the storm – like lightning, I struck!
Adversely stuck; the hearse, I ducked.
Everything but the most forbidden, I bucked.
How'd you do it?

Why'd you do it? Hope for nothing? Feeling in the dark?
Reaching for something just to find my heart empty and cold;
Packed up, moved out, and already sold?
From sunset to dawn – when the rooster crowed…
Thunder rolled but your love flowed.
If the story could unfold and be told…

Tell me…How'd you do it?

How'd it all start falling apart?
I, experimenter of life; master at no art.
When did the walls turn black and the halls go dark?
When did our trees grow sour leaves? Skinned in acrid bark?
When did these waters get crowded with bitter sharks?
Did your love for me really break your heart?
If so…How'd you do it?

How'd you put up with it? Where'd you carry it all?
Where'd you find the strength to carry it all?
How'd you escape the fall of trying to break my fall?
How'd you shake the earth quaking? –
Without shaking from all the aching? –
Without turning around, turning away, and escaping?
Without forsaking me?

WALTER H. MARTIN-EL

And your devotion to me which I didn't deserve?
    DAMN! I had some nerve!
So, how'd you do it?

    I'll probably never know how you did it –
Stayed so committed;
    Stepped to the plate, looked at the ball, -
Hit it.
    You didn't play with it;
You never half-stepped; never bullshitted.
    You could have quit it when I refused to quit it.
So, I have to admit it…
I thank God, thank you, and I'll never forget it!

THERE'S THIS WOMAN…

Here I am: unpopular to the world
And yet, she admires me.
There's this Woman…who somehow, without effort
Motivates and inspires me.
There's this Woman…who makes it look easy
No matter what she approaches or tackles;
Rises above negativity, pressures, and struggles;
Not perturbed by discouraging shackles.
Man, I love this woman!
How can I not love a woman such as this
Excuse me Miss –
May I lasso you with my ropes of affection
And engage you with my loving kiss?
She climbed every wall,
Jumped every obstacle and leaped every mountain.
Some days brought pain; many nights brought rain.
And tears flowed from her well like a fountain.

There's this Woman…that I love.
Whose smile seems to heal my every pain.
There's this Woman…who keeps me sane
When my sanity's hard to maintain.
There's this Woman…who loves me when I don't deserve it.
Now that's hard to explain.
Again – there's my love for this Woman –
Circulating inside of me from vein to vein.
There's this woman…whom I adore
And whose adoration for me is illustrated and graphic.
Our hearts seem to communicate
Through this bond which appears telepathic.
Whether over coffee or in traffic,

She shows strength; that of a maverick.
    She's cut from a rare cloth
That consists of strong thread and thick fabric.

    There's this Woman…who distilled patience
And held her head up with a smile.
    With me – She marched that extra mile.
I never understood how!
    There's this Woman…I loved ever since I was a kid.
And nothin' said Lovin' or brought heaven to our oven
Quite like she did.
    Watching steam escape through the lid
As she dabbed at the sweat on her face,
    I swore she knew magic.
Because everything she cooked disappeared without a trace.
    Amazing! – This Woman's grace!
So remarkable! – This Woman's elegance!
    I'll love her – Heart and Soul –
Till her hair is gray as thirty elephants.
    (and then some!)

    There's this Woman…
None other than my sweet, loving mother;
    She's been through more than her average share;
Survived! – That's why I love her!
    This is that Woman:
That I never would have made it without.
    This is that Woman…
All along, I serenaded about.
    Sensational Woman! – Inspirational Queen! –
Lovely, Beautiful, and Sweeter than sixteen.
    She loved me for being her son When society hated me for
being its felon.
    There's this Woman…
I would like to introduce to the world as my Mother.
Her name is Ellen - The First Lady of my Breath).

NOT IN LOVE?

So, you're not in love and never meant a word you said?
You can't imagine the evils that are flowing through my head.
I was so real and in return, you were so fake.
My, have I danced with a devil and romanced a cold snake.

So, my heart was a toy?
And playing with my feelings was a sport?
No matter how much I gave,
I still came up short.

What an ungrateful acquaintance
And selfish person you are.
But when you fall,
You can believe that I won't be far.

I'll be right there;
Not to catch you but to push you some more.
It's time I walk out the door
Before I decide to even the score.

What made me so vulnerable?
That I fell for your pitch?
Once I gave up my heart,
The script was flipped and the channel got switched.

I'll never believe another solitary word you speak.
And now I'm about to turn the tables;
While playing humble and weak.

First, I'll turn the other cheek
And play by your rules.
You underestimated my wisdom
Just like all the other sorry fools.

I gave you a chance!
I gave you chance after chance to do the right thing.
   When you were just a puppet in my play
Dangling from a tight string.

   And now I shall cut that string
And stop all this pretending.
   The curtains are closing
And it won't be a happy ending.

   You play with life and death…
Not caring if you breathe or die.
   So, you're not in love anymore?
Well, I've got a confession:
Neither am I!

DEAR GOD

Dear God:

Please give me the strength to let go of everything I've been needlessly trying to hold on to. I really, really need you to remove me from this situation or remove this situation from me. I've been a friend to people who could never be friends to me. I've been forsaken and betrayed by those I've devoted my loyalty to. I'm disregarded by those I show my respect to. I'm not recognized for my integrity and chivalry. God, take the love out of my heart. Help me to let go of what I can't have or keep. Help me to distinguish between what belongs to me and what belongs to the world. Grant me more wisdom and teach me to find comfort and contentment in my serenity. Heal my mind, body, and emotions. This is my prayer.

Dear God:

Brethren partake in supper and break bread at the same table with me. The bitter taste of betrayal steams from a dish right in front of me. And I want to regurgitate every bite of disloyalty that grinded between my clenching teeth and cut my gums like forkfuls of broken glass. Protect and shield me from my own heart and my good nature. Enclose me in a clear mind. God, You surround me with the characters in order that You may construct and institute character in me. You did a great job. This is my prayer.

Dear God:

Thank You for the ability to forgive the things that won't forget to hurt me again and again. Enlarge my capacity to grasp what You give me when I can't get a grip and when I see no need to hold on. Thank You for the sight to see that I've always, (until now), been blind to the vision in Your will. I build walls around myself to keep me from traveling my greatest distance. Thank You for using those walls to teach me how to climb to my highest potentials. They don't know that at my best, I can't fall. I didn't know that, as long as I *think* I'm at my highest, I can't rise. Hold me together when I want to crumble to pieces. Hold me close when I want to stumble away. Walk with me through a life where all the others walked out on me. I had wounded feelings that needed healing. You delivered me through my passion and strength. You changed my heart, my mind, my attitude, my life. Life captured me so You could release me. Now give me the courage and the spirit of Joseph to say, ***"FORGIVEN!"*** This is my prayer, dear God!

TROUBLED (LIFE)

Okay, I said it!
I'm troubled in a troubled way.
I got on my mother's nerves.
So she would say to me, "Go play!"
I'll go play alright…
As soon as I get to school tomorrow.
I don't steal from her purse.
Sometimes I just get the urge to borrow.
Hold on! – Who are those guys at the end of the block?
I like the way those hats look when they're slightly cocked.
I want to hold that glock – Pops had a forty-five.
Pops was bad and he kept a sporty ride – his glory and pride.
They look at me and say,
"Shorty bad as hell! But Shorty live!"
This is a story about how Shorty strived…
To survive one "friend" with forty knives –
All aimed at his back
Like hornets from ruffled nests and trouble hives.
Trouble in his life – But before he hides,
He'll gloat; he'll glide across the bubbled tides.
Everyone has an angel and a smile with a million sides.
My father was no angel – I know because he told a million lies.
The less he tried,
I didn't give a…because the less I cried!
Yes, my life's a troubled mess.
And how'd you guess?
It's no puzzle he died.

IF YOU WERE IN MY SHOES…

If you were in my shoes, you would love you too.
My love for you will end all pain
other brothers took you through.
If you were in my shoes, could you stand in my place?
Laces tied just in case
You have to fight to keep what's yours?
If you were in my shoes, would you pace the floors?
When it seemed your heart closed its doors?
If you were in my shoes, I think you would see…
That it's easy loving you – But it's hard being me.

It's only one thing harder than being in love. That is being in love with someone who isn't in love with you as much as you are in love with them.

Just like any and all other emotions, love is one that must be conquered and subdued or else it will consume one whole.

Loving someone who doesn't feel they deserve to be loved could be overpowering and exhausting because they won't know how to reciprocate the love.

Love is an entity that must be first learned, next taught, then shared. And this is the place where the inspiration for this poem was born.

WHAT CAUGHT MY EYE

I remember the first day I saw you and what caught my eye.
My flirtatious glance took a trip from your calf to your thigh.
I was trippin' Baby – hopin' I could get those legs to spread –
Like rich, creamy peanut butter on soft wheat bread.
Visions of me exploring you danced in my head.
Then it happened! – You were lying yo' sexy self
Right there in my bed.
I'm talkin' 'bout the same night.
I was like, "Dayum, my game tight!"
Alright, alright!... it was destiny.
And timing was definitely right!
(But we ain't even do nothin')
Your naiveness caught my eye;
I knew you had never been loved.
That alone challenged me to wanna carry you above…
The same non-sense, riff-raff; one night stands.
If life meant for us to be together,
Who am I to shun life's plans?
My left hand took your right hip in a firm, tight grip.
We needed a, 'wet floor' sign that said, "CAUTION!"
"You might slip!"
From leaking to pouring down rain,
Then back to a slight drip;
I'm thinking the mattress might rip.
We can't help but to bite lips.
(But that's a whole 'nother story).

You wanna know what caught my eye?
Like a pop-fly in a catcher's glove?
It was when I first saw those dimples
And I almost needed two stretchers my love!

I said to myself, "Self, she wants you –
Just as bad as you want her."
    Instantaneously, my mind started to whir.
And my emotions started to stir.

    Today, I've still never met a woman with your moan.
I never would've guessed that with you I'd feel so alone.
(But I messed up!)

    You're what caught my eye.
I'm not cunning you with schemes.
    I swear it's the truth!
You've been running through my dreams.

    The moments; the memories; all the magic we shared;
Your forgiveness when I behaved as if I never cared.

    When the stages of our love was still elementary.
You opened your heart and body and gave me "hella-entry".
    Access to who you are and your vulnerability. Then, I wasn't
a man. But here's my display of humility.
(I'm sorry!)

    My Queen is what caught my eye:
The Woman and Soul-mate I was bound to find.
    Down the line you made me a King.
The cause and effect of my crown and its shine.

    We weren't together long enough.
I'm hoping eternity might be found.
    Because if I don't want to spend the rest of my life with you,
May Allah strike me down.

    May lightning strike me now!
And run away with my life.
    That's if you make me live without you…

Instead of being my wife.
(Will you marry me?)

People have hurt me in ways
You never would have hurt me.
I thought I'd never love you like this.
It took the essence in you to convert me.
You know how to entice me, then work me,
(Damn! I miss your touch!)

Here's what caught my eye…
How I let what was supposed to be our life together
Waltz right by.
You thought, 'Why try?' – 'Why cry?' Why lie?
Twas my fault. I thought...I'd die!

When I actually realized you'd slipped through my fingers.
Tell me you still want me; need me; that the desire still lingers;
That no man can make you feel the way I make you feel;
That what bonds us is still real and stronger than steel.

I'll get down on bended knees.
Where do you want me to kneel?
I don't want to be the reason you hurt.
I want to be the reason you heal.
(Shh…Let me fix it.)

I was taught that 'Beauty' is in the eye of the beholder. I've come to understand this to mean that beauty is indescribable. Because a one, universal definition for beauty does not exist.

No two people have seen beauty from the same perspective. Beauty is not what always catches the eye. It is the essence and spirit within what appears beautiful. And when that essence / spirit of beauty does catch the eye, the whole eye becomes as beautiful as that which it sees. And the beholder becomes the same.

TEACH AND REMIND

God placed me in the war with the wounded –
To teach me to fight.
And become sensitive to the afflictions of the scarred.
He placed me in the shadow of the sick –
To teach and remind me to heal the infirmities of the ill.
He surrounded me with the weakness of the weakest –
To teach and remind me of my power –
To be the strength of the strongest.
He progressed me among the oppressed, fearful,
Scared, and afraid – to raise me up in might.
And polish me with the courage to conquer and overcome.
He poured me and stirred me into a pot of boiling chaos –
To teach me to command and demand **PEACE** –
The storm is still.
He conceived me in '**NOT**' to unite, unfold,
and birth me into what 'becomes' – and from my tongue
first came the words, "Let there **BE!**"
He molded me in silence – to teach me His language:
How to communicate where to converse with Him.
He would teach me to expose the knowledge of God,
Is to expose the ignorance of self.
He carved His precepts on the brick walls of my prisons –
To teach and remind me of my freedom of existence
And the inevitable existence of my freedom.
No cares; no worries; no depression –
No insecurities must invade the battle grounds of my thought:
Only self-reflections and outward expressions…
Of God in me and I in Him.
He educated me while in the state of worldly confusion –
To show me the evil in misunderstanding existence.
And the evil existence of misunderstanding.

God united me with His universe;
Added me to His animate inventions:
He multiplied my possibilities;
Conjoining them with the unthinkable –
And rested me in the neighborhoods of my enemies –
To teach me and remind me that…
In the ***DIE-VISION of my people the VISION DIES!***
He blessed me with the dying thirst for the knowledge of self
In a deserted desert and a dry wilderness –
To teach and remind me that –
To learn me is to Love you!
He made me different –
To teach and remind me that we are the same and together.
We change! We evolve!
He gave me one hand to save my self.
He gave me my other hand to teach and remind me –
To save and deliver you from the many hands of the adversary.
He reminds me of where I was to show me that,
Where I am, will teach me in what direction to head next.
From the darkest tunnels of the heart –
Which funnels light to the golden streets of PURIFIED speech –
Comes the waters of life that extinguishes the fiery flames
Of mind's hell.
He constantly reminds me of the heat from this hell.
He sterilizes me with the burns thereof, to teach me that –
The understanding that stands after the ashes of ignorance
Have been swept away…and is the instructions for
The building and the construction of Heaven-in-man.
Every test is a lesson taught.
And every trial and tribulation is a reminder that –
In Him, I can fail at no thing!
And NO disaster which may come upon me and against me,
Can overtake me! – Prosperously!
Oh how He has broken me, only to make me ***Unbreakable!***
He planted my feet high on the three step ladder of salvation –

Only to forsake me? – Please!
No matter the torrent, my belief is unwavering;
No matter the wind, my faith is still; Fixed; Unmovable!
No matter the thundering, my fruition is unshakable!
I Am Truth! – Absolute!; Unmistakable!
Upon me and somewhere within me is falsehood:
A 'temporary' overcome by infinity. – Unfathomable!
Self has yet to enter the imagination of man.
To him, 'nothing' is something…
And God in him is unimaginable.
(Now ain't that something?')
What is life? – But one experience after another?
What is this world? – But the outcome and conditions
Of these same experiences?
What am I to learn? – But that I am just passing through –
On a journey back to where time never existed.
This knowledge and wisdom is resisted as if restricted. (Is it?)
On this plane God will teach me what I must be taught;
Remind me that without a doubt, I must be reminded –
Reminded that, so as earth is – so it is with man.
So as nature is – so it is with the disposition of man:
Temperamental.
Anything I've forgotten
Is everything I've never considered worth learning.
In this, I am reminded to consider all things.
The One who sees all things teaches me to look
Through the eyes of God and see through the eyes of men and
observe that…
As I strive to become divinity manifested in matter,
I strive harder to become matter manifested in divinity.
With the spirits of the force of thought,
The Most Divine lives in my power to create life
In a world that is an illusion…
Which is a world that can be taught and reminded –
Of what again?

UNFORGETTABLE

So Unforgettable – As unforgettable can get.
How can I forget? – When & how we met?
     As with any flight,
We experienced turbulence from the start.
     But it didn't take long
To notice the sweetness in her heart.
     Unforgettable was the first time I laid eyes on her.
I pondered – view never wandered – Damn! – I wanted her!

     Something about her really messed with my head.
She reminded me of the princess in every story book I read.
     First – we became friends; then special buddies.
From the kisses and the huggies – to X-Rated lovie-dovies.

     Caught up in the unforgettable moment;
Wrapped up in one another.
     Next came my son, then my daughter;
Thanks to their unforgettable mother.
     Life threw the curve that took me away from them.
Now I just pray for them – while she makes a way for them.

     Year after year – they're still growing.
From living with them to dying without them –
But I'm still going.
     Still taking punches the world's still throwing;
Showing no signs of these steel wheels slowing.

     She's been my Light and still glowing.
She's my ark – Noah's flood winds are still blowing.
     She gets mad respects! –
Representing for the shawties whose dad neglects.
     This dad regrets when his past reflects –
Lost, tender years when dads and young lads connect.

But she stepped up! –
Doing what ***all real*** women would:
Became that one, Hell-u-va woman
That battled and withstood.
Now that's Unforgettable!
She gave birth to my child.
She's my princess and Madonna.
I'll love her no matter what
Comes of life's dramas.
I compliment her to the fullest: My Confidant and Lover.
I congratulate her for being so unforgettable.
And I didn't stutter.

THE HONEST DEFINITION OF
A TRUE WOMAN

Can she honestly be described, pin-pointed, and defined?
Got a name? – Some form of I.D. I can locate or find?
Can she be wined and dined by a regular type of guy?
Would she mind if I tested her with my stare?
Miss Candy – Too sweet for the eye!?
The honest definition of a true woman's
whatever a man thinks.
He could gaze at her for hours
With no blinks.
Truly amazed at her selection –
from her shape to her complexion;
Easy to approach.
And upon contact's an immediate connection.
Her affection is pure and natural;
she's perfect and complete:
From her weight to her height –
From her head to her feet.
A true woman knows my space –
Not insecure about her place
She's sexy! –
Whether there's a tear or a smile on her face.
A true woman breathes meaning.
She bears a purpose on this earth.
Although her physical attributes –
Are not all that she's worth.
A true woman is always recognized
For recognizing a true man.
Acknowledged – for her charismatic disposition –
Well composed – cool as a fan.
In the field of love and devotion – true women are experts.

A true woman will love a true man until her chest hurts.
   She remains dedicated. She'd never leave my side.
She wouldn't scornfully betray me.
She isn't caught up in her pride.
   The honest definition of a true woman is one such as this:
She knows how I want to be treated; how I want to be touched –
Kissed.
   She respects herself!
She is certain and confident in all she does.
   I learned – The honest definition of a true woman –
When I saw what the imitation was.
   She's warm and caring; sensitive to all my needs.
When I'm hurting, tears catapult from her cheeks –
And in her heart, she bleeds.
   A true woman keeps our secrets personal;
She values my trust.
   She's honest and virtuous –
Revealing her innocence in her blush.
   She honors her relationships; her nature is to love.
Not expecting what she doesn't deserve –
Giving her all when push comes to shove.
   She's adventurous and not afraid – She's perfectly made.
She's my sunlight and shade; my help meet and my aide.
   She's every part of me when we're together –
Or separated and apart.
   These words have been copied from the pages of my heart.
Because my woman is the definition of a true woman.

A SOLITAIRE BROTHER'S PLEA

May the Angels in Heaven celebrate the day of your birth.
There isn't enough gold at the end of God's rainbow
That could amount to your value and worth.

You've always been truly remarkable;
An outstanding member of our domestic hearth.
To get to 'LOVE', you'll walk across fire and burning
brimstone – Replenishing life with joy unspeakable –
In its areas of extreme dearth.

You've been a tree which is someone's strength.
Sweet like brown maple – with a fragrance like mirth.
When I was in the alleys and valleys –
Your prayers were my protection on this earth.

This world is like a razor-edged sword.
And people cut you like blades from the sharpest knives.
But you're a shining star that lights up the firmaments
And the skies – shining through the darkest lives.
I've been to a place that no man can go.
Unless, of course, he dies.
I've been victimized; fighting to open my eyes –
Only to find that my blessing cries.
You might not know. But you're a blessing in disguise.
When we embrace I know heaven's in my hand.
After the clouds and the rains – you'll be my shelter –
On dry land – My castle in my sand.
I've been stabbed in my back;
Hurt, wounded, bleeding, abandoned – trying to stumble free.
You spoke softly to my heart words of solace and peace.
You inspired me and humbled me.
You've been my courage and motivation.

You've been the perseverance in me that thrives.
    You're what Solomon searched for in 300 concubines.
And about 700 wives.
    I was tangled in the webs of the streets –
Shopping in the gutters for what might destroy me utterly.
    When poisoned by the venom of the curious spider –
You were my rescue and therapeutic recovery.
    Pain and tribulation had emotionally crippled me.
Your battles made you patient and forbearing.
    I was unaware of what God was preparing.
My heart was being torn and you warned me of more tearing –
So damn unconditionally caring!

    Through the most frigid and coldest blizzards –
Your love and concern is the fire that kept me warm.
    You gave me the guts to stomach the turbulence.
Your spirit and smile is my comfort in the eye of the storm.
    Be proud of yourself – Who you are –
Of your accomplishments. You came a long way.
    When the song of adversity aired, you suffered long –
Knowing it was okay to just let the song play.
    God made you strong!
The Potter would never, ever use the wrong clay!
    You were never too weak to fall on your knees.
I'm one who believes that only the strong pray.
    When I look at you I see someone extraordinary
and special. And I know in my heart –
That's exactly what others see.
    Whatever you do – don't change or give up on me.
Always keep loving me!-
This is a solitaire brother's plea.

IF YOU LOVE ME…

If you love me, love me again. And tomorrow, tell me you love me more than you loved me yesterday. Then, tell me again like I've never heard you say it before today. If you've ever loved me, then don't stop loving me now.

If you love me, trust me. Love and trust will never disagree with one another. They are intimately bonded and closely related. Neither can thrive, survive, or exist without the other existing.

If you love me, have faith in me with your every element. When you look at me, stare at me and observe me with that trusting love in your eyes. Every time you close those trust-filled eyes, fall in love with me all over again.

Love has no face but many bodies. *If you love me,* don't hate me when your love for me makes you angry at me. *If you love me,* don't give up on me when a confused love confuses your believing and forgiving heart. *If you love me,* keep trying. Because love won't cease to make advances or search for solutions.

Love loves to expect the unexpected. And *if you love me,* You won't expect me to be perfect. Love will remember that I'm not perfect while loving me like I already am perfected and perfectly polished with a perfect love that shines through a seemingly, perfect darkness.

A perfect love is a love with nothing missing and nothing stolen. Is your love for me a perfect one? Is our love a perfect one?

If you love me, you're going to smile like Heaven does for a returning Angel – as if your smile was the emotional sunshine that gives our relationship the light and energy it hungers and thirsts for to flourish.

If you love me, your heart will cry those tear drops of joy that will fall into the flower pots of our romance where the stalk and stem of our relationship first budded and began blossoming.

If you love me, you'll struggle through the dirt with me, against the weeds of disloyalty and unfaithfulness as we sprout together to a mature state of growth and solid camaraderie.

If you love me, you'll love me against all odds; against all unfavorable; against all naysayers. Your love would be with me and not against me. You would love me to depend on your love for any and everything.

Love is true; nothing and nowhere close to a lie. Love will not promise what it can not deliver or has no intentions on delivering.

If you love me, you'll have my best interests at heart. And matters of my heart would matter most of all to you.

Love is never rehearsed. Love is authentic and behaves in 'automatic' mode. Love is spontaneous and doesn't plan. But love for me should always be in your plan as it is always in my plan for you.

I love you and I am more than willing to take the necessary approaches and go through the proper channels to re-tie and re-knot the ropes of our valued, long-time affection. *If you love me,* you'll be eager to let me.

What we've commissioned the hands of love to create and develop required hardships and invested longsuffering.

We lit a flame and set a bond on fire that shouldn't be so easily and quickly defused, smothered, or extinguished.

If you love me, you won't hate me due to small arguments. In the blaze of disagreement, words can be intense, strong, and painful.

Truth is, they hurt tremendously! But that's only when they're being spoken from deep within the wells of pain which is always one's temporary weakness.

Because I love you, I am truly understanding and sympathetic to the intense emotions and feelings that I can, only through love, detect and decipher through your spirit.

Therefore, I surrender you, my Love, these feelings of mine to reflect the illustrated images of my loving thoughts; that you may explore the expressions of my sentiments as well as allow me to caress and massage your pains with meek consideration.

Don't allow your irritations to mold you merciless.

We have to let love teach us to be stronger than our strongest demons. We have to, through the strength of our love, overcome, overpower, and conquer the assaults on our love by everybody and everything visible and invisible that doesn't want our love to be real love. *If you love me*, you'll read that last sentence again.

If you love me, you'll allow love to initiate positive ideas in order to alleviate negative vibes and stimulations. We are going to go through – just as well as our love has already been through – some tempestuous storms. But our love can't allow the rains to wash away the precious garden in which we've been planting seeds of forever in for what seems to have been an eternity.

If you love me, you won't let our separation cripple our closeness. Our continuous love must be the therapeutic remedy that livens and revives our romance when it starts fading and withering. And that 'thing' we have for one another starts dying.

Before either one of us becomes rash and makes an irrational decision that is dangerous to our love, we must blanket ourselves with peaceful memories and memorable moments as well as cuddle with good thoughts of one another. We must tell ourselves that we wouldn't do it any other way if we indeed loved the other.

If you love me, you'll learn me. You'll know me and you'll never forget me. You would understand love; your love as your love understands me.

If you love me, you'll take cover in the binding bond and freedom of our connection when doubt launches and says that my love for you is weak or fraudulent.

If you love me, you won't penalize me for the mistakes I can't take back. Instead you will encourage me to be courageous enough to move forward and past those mistakes and be strong enough not to make the same ones again. You will improvise and compromise when we find ourselves trapped in high, gusty winds of misunderstanding and miscommunication.

If you love me, you'll notice my smiles and not be discouraged, dismayed, or disheartened by my frowns of frustrations and periods of sadness.

If you love you me, you'll realize that your bad dreams about our bad times are just fluttering butterflies of anticipated excitement about our good times and more good times to come. They're also misinterpretations of the true passions that you possess for this thing called, "US". They are false images of what tomorrow won't bring. Nor is it fair to label those bad dreams as law or paint them as permanent portraits of our present, non-pleasurable misfortune or soon-to-be unfortunate end.

If you love me, your love will be complete, assuring me that you are completely in love with me and that our togetherness will continue to ferment and never be incomplete, discontinued, or destroyed.

If you love me, your love will be fervent and unconditional, but never partial or bias. Love will remind and advise you that we've already been friends; that we will always be friends; that the word, *'only',* in *'only friends',* doesn't have enough letters to spell out what more destiny has in store for us and our love.

If you love me, you won't break my heart. Your love would be thorough.

Love is a law that can't be broken. It is a rule that can't be bent, changed, or revised. *If you love me,* you'll enforce the rule and law of love. You'll believe our love was written.

Love is like see-through glass; cutting sharp and deep when it is shattered: A hexagon of many prisms and dimensions that symbolizes the versatility of our love.

Love will give you the chills while in the heart of the scorching heat of desire. Love will moisten you with a cold sweat when the warmth of our chemistry turns cold. But love won't freeze up.

If you love me, every time you tell me you love me, you'll start all over again making me feel loved all over again just so you could tell me you love me – all over again.

I want to spend the rest of my life drinking from the wells, the springs, the jars, and basins of our love – forever drunk and intoxicated off of your splendor and beauty.

Love will make you nauseous and sick when you can't figure out the way.

Love will heal you when you're dying inside from the quiet afflictions of love pangs. True love feels good even when everything else hurts.

Love is not invisible. *If you love me,* your love can't possibly be, 'Out of sight; Out of mind'. Love is: Going out of your rabbit-ass-mind when I'm out of your sight.

If you love me, absence and distance wouldn't persuade you to be absent and distant from me. Love would keep you right in my reach so that when I reach out for your love, my grasp is not denied.

Certain feelings in your heart can mislead you, misguide you, and misdirect you by luring you towards the wrong direction. However, our love is there to steer your heart and true love is concentrated on, *'who and what'* – not, *'when', 'where', 'why',* or *'how'.* Therefore, *if you love me,* you won't listen to or be changed by the chaos in your heart. You'll listen to the still voice of what is still love.

Love is past, present, and future. Because love is inspirationally prophetic. Love shows us what the future will bring – only if you're not blind – ignoring the love for me that is breathing in you.

If you love me, you'll look past my shortcomings and see that I love you through thick and thin. You'll be compassionate to two things: 1.) I need you! 2.) I want and desire you with my every iota of affection.

Without you, I am unplugged and without power. *If you love me,* you won't make me stop loving you and you won't make yourself stop loving me.

Love doesn't have to force anything.
Because love is a force of its own.
And what it owns came naturally.

Love can not be separated. So why should we be? How could we be outside of the physical?
Because love is whole and not in parts.

If you love me, you won't concentrate on the fact that I may not have ever expected this much from you or expressed myself in this manner before. Oh Angelic Love of mine, that doesn't matter once real love takes the stage.

I want love to sweep out old corners and open up new areas of our hearts that we've never occupied. I want love to snuggle in your crevices that you've never exposed to me.

Before you try something new with yourself or with someone else, try something new with 'US'! That's *if you love me.* That's if you love, "US"!

Try something new with our love. Be willing to let love work it out.

I love you! I truly need to truly love you - So I can make you feel like you're first in my life and perfect for my life.
Precious, don't ever again say, "Good-bye," to what you love. Don't say, "Good-bye," to what we have yet to say, "Hello," to, welcome, and expect next. Love isn't over!

If you love me, you'll read this again!

OUR LOVE WILL MAKE IT!

No matter the storms or how much of the rains that come down; the thunders may roar and lightning may strike the ground…

Our love will make it above the face of the waters and not drown; when everything else is washed away, our love will still be found…

No matter the punches or the blows that the arm of this life throws; if no one else knows, we know – That our love will make it!

No matter how cold or if the whole world froze—

Through degrees in the highest of highs and the lowest of lows—

Our love will make it!

Trials and tribulations may test our love…from this very moment until the rest of our love!

Yet our love will make it. Because blessed is our love!

When worse meets worst – The best is the best of our love!

When down, our love will get up - When weary, never give up.

It will endure this race until it ends.

Our love will fight with all its strength and its might -

Even if it runs against the four seasons and the four winds.

Sometimes it seems like the end has come;

Like nothing else can be done - But our love will make it!

The bond of our love was built with the tools of perfection - By the hands of God -

And there is no way possible that human holds can break it!

So no matter what we go through - And we don't know what else to do

Look in the pockets of our heart; Find the wallet of love and embrace it.

If bad or good, down or up, in or out -
There is no 'one' without the 'two'.
But through it all and no matter what - Just believe in our love-

And our love will make it!

HAS ANYONE SEEN GOD?

Pregnant woman missing: Last seen – She wore jeans.
Found dead in an abandoned building: Four teens on morphine.
When we return: Live from Katrina –
Stay tuned for more scenes.
Has anyone seen God?
I have a message from New Orleans.

West Nile's a pest now – Pesky lil' insect – WOW!
She's eight with breasts now - So hubby molests child.
Police suspects pal 'cause Mom protects cow –
Who injured her baby – For life! – And his sweat's foul!
Detect's inspects file, connects style, and necks bow.
In the Globe – 'Father caught on his next prowl'.

Has anyone seen God? – Virginia Tech's on line one.
H.I.V.'s on line two – holding hostage a dying son.
My country's committing suicide –
Plotting on more schemes:
Rotten to the core; wounded and sore.
And the sore stings!
Iraqi needs thorazine – so it seems – And Darfur screams!
Has anyone seen God? – Has he seen what the poor dreams?

Why hasn't He intervened in the East -
Where the war steams?
The door swings – And there's 'Life' –
Yet, attached to more strings.
Poor thing! – Born addicted to 'crack'
And with poor genes.
Has anyone seen the devil?
Tell'em to give us back the Lord's wings!

GOD LIVES IN THE GHETTO

Screeching tires; Burning rubber;
Skid marks on the concrete;
Pot-holes; there another car goes –
Across broken glass in the street.
Welcome to the ghetto where God sleeps past the dawn.
In the suburbs, his eyes are open at sunrise –
Because he has to mow the lawn.
Here – this King becomes a pawn:
Recognized for his sacrifice and labors.
He's commended –
For his love, concern, and sudden respect for his neighbors.
But they really don't like him.
They see the strength in which he's empowered.
They want him to move back to the ghetto – Where the
goddess sleeps next to this coward.
Back to the place where God's face frowns on many souls;
Where it's cool to drive Chevies, Cutlasses, and Bonnevilles –
Full of bullet holes.
God sleeps in the ghetto: Deaf to the cries of burning metal.
He wakes up in the suburbs from the nightmares
Of blood left on his curbs.
In the suburbs, it's, 'peaches and cream'; 'cookies and herbs';
Proper English: Adjectives, nouns, and verbs.
In the ghetto, it's 'slang': "Don't make me pop this thang!"
God's eyes are closed and his sleep is not disturbed.
He's chased by his own feet; He's cornered and trapped.
In the suburbs he awakes from his nap –
And feels no need to stay strapped.
He's tightly wrapped, well behaved, and suddenly composed;
Pants pulled up; shirt tucked – And where'd he get those clothes?
In the ghetto – Where God sleeps…

There's no hope for the son of this God.
    And what place is more suitable to relax,
Get comfortable, and take a nod?
    Does it not seem odd that tragedy weighs in by the tons?
If Moses split the red sea with a rod –
What does God need with sooooo many guns?
    In the ghetto he bathes in bloody rags.
In the suburbs he waves his white flags.
    He once carried a 'piece' – Now he's married to 'PEACE'.
His shorts no longer sag from the weight of those tiny, little bags.
    In the ghetto, he stays hard.
He says it's because his way's hard.
    Somebody shake God! – Awake God!
He sleeps in his own graveyard.
    He's a security guard?
In the suburbs God watches for the burglar?
    But back in the ghetto, God was a drug dealer.
And a cold-blooded murderer.
    If God possesses the earth and its riches –
Why does he kill for money?
    What is it about the suburbs?
That land of milk and white honey?
    Grass is green; streets are smooth –
This moves his fascination.
    He's the heart of the ghetto:
Its expectation and emancipation.
    The suburbs extended no invitation –
But the suburb is his inspiration.
    He's not welcome –
Where the wealthy and financially healthy
Leave their doors unlocked.
    Sure, he keeps his music down now. But here's the problem:
No black girls live on this block.
    Who will he marry? How will he reproduce?
If he even looks at Mother-Goose, he'll find his neck in a noose.

Oh, did I mention that God was a black man?
He smokes Newports: The 'black's' brand.
　　The 'white' man spits where the blacks stand.
Because he can't survive where the blacks can.
　　And if he shakes a black's hand, believe me,
it's just an act man.
　　He doesn't want your burnt feet to stand –
On his precious, white sand.
　　But God is a sleep-walker. When he falls he sleep-crawls.
Instead of God being all-knowing, God is a cold know-it-all.
　　God created war in the ghetto.
And he sheds blood by the pools.
　　In the suburbs, he follows all the rules;
Can't wait to send his kids to all the 'white' schools.
　　He refers to his sister as, 'BITCH'!
He'll smack his mother and sell her 'crack'.
　　Pull a pistol on his brother –
And go a little further to steal the shirt off of his back.
　　From, "Whaz crackin'?" – to, "Lez git it poppin'!"
And, "What choo got on a bar-b-que?"
　　To, "Hi, how do you do?"
And, "Here, This is for you."
　　Yeah, I know it's hard to view. But it's simple.
It's evident and very easy to see.
　　When I speak of this god, his residence; his relevance –
I'm speaking of you and me.
　　We hate those that love us –
And love those that hate our very flesh.
　　Why? – Because God sleeps in the ghetto
And I think you know the rest!

I DON'T NEED YOU!

Just to tell me what you think I want to hear?
Taking deep breaths to exhale ferocious lies that blow me away?
You know me today? But tomorrow…
You just throw me away?
I don't need you!

When the storm winds are strong – I'm weak; you're gone!
You tell me to just hold on…To what? – And for how long?
When all goes wrong…every time:
With everything and everyone…
Where are you? – *I don't need you!*
No, I don't need you now!

Even when you're present, you're still not with me.
Through the unbearable and unpleasant you seem to forget me.
But I'm always am – In all ways, never forgotten:
An endowment of life – left to rot; yet life not rotten.
I don't need you!

You were just trying to protect me
From the evil that men do?
Who shall protect me –
From the evil which is within in you?
Am I he who should defend you?
Love me with undying, unconditional love?
You couldn't even possibly pretend to.
I don't need you!

What can kill me but nothing?
Not even by weapons that are made by hand.
I fear not the last seconds of 'life'.
Because they were made by man.

Show me these 'last moments' of 'life'.
And I'll show you that life is…Indescribable of time.
     "This' is not my life – I AM THE LIFE –
Of whatever and everything this is;
The height of what you must find the strength to climb.
     Or fall into an impetuous , inconclusive failing.
I stand bare-feet on the sea of infinity:
Strong-legged and still sailing.
I don't need you!

     So hails away! Be that ship that sails away!
Because you're that last straw;
I'm the barn filled with bails of hay!
Back up! – *I don't need you!*
     You search for treasures and pleasures.
But I am that jewel and what's pleasurable.
     I am that which defies distance and weight –
An extension beyond mortal reason.
     From the smallest eye to the biggest 'I', I'm immeasurable.
I don't need you!

     I need 'I'…Once deceived by 'me' and possessed by 'my'.
You're still stressed and getting depressed? You still cry? Why?
     Come on now! I thought you had it all together.
I learned to carry the weight of the world –
As if it were as light as a feather.
I don't need you!

     When I gotta travel through the pain –
You can't carry my bags.
     Across sun-burnt gravel; through ice-cold rain –
You're not worth a dog or the tail he wags.
     But I hear you growlin'.
Because I glow like the light of the moon?
Is that why you're howlin'?
     Barking up the wrong tree?
These lyrics were trapped. But now I set this song free.
     And I will sing it to you with the bass of the sky's thunder!

SURPRISE! I am a disguised wonder!
But you and your promises are equal –
To that substance which flies plunder.
And yo' shit don't stank?

I don't need you to clasp on to my wings –
Just to pull me under –
To the mountain's peak of your misery and hell.
My words crushed you like the heaviness of water –
When dams fell.
God knows my heart's as flawless -
As the pearl inside the clam's shell.
Our head-on collision will be the story two rams tell.
Though meek as a lamb, I will not be heard like the lamb's bell…
When I tell you… *I don't need you!*

Shut in, shut out, and shut up –
I will conquer until my open wounds are closed shut.
Take caution at attempting to crack this shell.
Because once done, you'll be in the company of an exposed nut!
Who knows what? – May unfold?
But a mystery like eighteen years of Jesus' life untold?
Like a room filled with innocent children…
When a gun unloads?
I may fire and then fire and then misfire –
Until hers, yours, and his tire –
Is empty of that air of envy that suffocates me.
All because you hate yourself soooo much, you hate me?
Now I break free from your clutch…and lately…
I'm un-clutchable and out of your reach.
Just you entering my thoughts –
Constitutes a trespass and a breech –
Of my partial existence.
You beseech. But I am persistently impartial with resistance.
Because… *I don't need you!*

I am detached from our attachment;
Disinterested in what was once interesting.
Being compassionate to you…
Where there was no compassion for me…
Hasn't been the best thing!
Dispassionate – to the passions once felt;
No longer standing, shining, or burning once the wax melts.
Neutral to the positives as well as the negatives;
The 'some-times', like-minded – And other times…competitive-(s).
Not involved mentally, spiritually, or emotionally –
With our involvement.
No longer impressed and am patiently anticipating…
The imminent…*I don't need you!*

I am now well and no longer repugnant by the quell
Of our intimacy.
Now let the vessel and the soul –
Which is fenced in this and be free…
Of the rickety chords of our weakness;
Your insecurities, un-sureties, and bleakness!
Let your pessimism be the evidence of your hope to fail –
And your failure to hope – Then ask yourself…
"Who needs you?"
I Don't!

You can dupe the world, beguile yourself,
But fool me twice when once you already have?
Pretend like you're not smiling at my aches and sufferings?
Must I remind you? – You already laughed?
Church can't save you and God doesn't know you.
And since you don't know God or yourself –
I don't trust you as far as I can throw you!
And what you do behind my back? –
I can slap you right in the face for!
But you're clue-less, out of place

And somewhere my world just isn't a place for:
    Disgusting, detestable, indigestible –
Something I no longer have the taste for.
    You defile creation –
The reason the Creator should erase more.
    Please forgive me – Not! –
If forgiving you is something I've declined to do.
    And if this is a hard pill to swallow…
Just choke instead of trying to chew.
    Because living to see me dying –
Has always been something you've been dying to do!
    Although you won't stop lying to me –
I won't start lying to you – The truth is –
I don't need you!!!!!!!

I'M COOL WITH IT

They want to know what it is about me –
That motivates me to move.
    When everyone else moves without me,
I just move how I move.
    And I just keep moving right along;
Moving up; moving ahead; moving about –
I'm cool with it.

    They want to see what it is about me:
What it is they ain't seeing that keeps causing them to doubt me.
    Oh…I see – They see what they want to see.
But if they see just a little bit,
They've already seen a bit too much.
    They just don't get it.
But…I'm cool with it.

    They can't figure me out.
I figure that's a good thing.
    Underestimate me? – I'm cool with that.
I'm cooler than zero degrees Celsius on the thermostat.
But what I do shouldn't concern no cat.
    Is it me? Or is it everyone else in the world?
    I'm a mess!
I'm a quest·ion – mark·ed with the impress·ion that:
    You understand 'one' thing about me – If you never know No
thing about me.
I could never learn your name and….I'm cool with that!

    They can't take their eyes off me!
They watch me as if caught in a spell.
    They're hypnotized by the Hell – That I raise –
After my shell's been raised and I'm in a whole 'notha phase –

On that ass! Hey, I'm cool with it.

Yall was cool with it –
When I wasn't acting a stone, plum fool with it.
See, I'm authentic;
That's why they break their necks to stay all in it:
My business that is!
But I'm not offended.
I already know they're soft-ended.
They're not hard around the edges –
Just burnt and charred around the edges.
I'm cool with it.

They've just got to deal with it. I'm real with it!
Because I'm the real game. I'm the real name.
They're all aliases:
Bad blood as if righteousness has blown by;
As if by-gones have gone by.
I must be – got to be 'the wrong guy'.
That's what I'm most non-affectionately known by.
And as crazy as this may sound,
They're all screaming they want to see me.
Yeah…They all want to see me dead and miserable!
I'm cool with it.

But *they* better be cool with it –
When harvest time matures;
When all those dead seeds and manure –
Come back to natural life that they may endure
That kind of sick payback that can't be cured.
Now are they cool with that? You sure?
Well…Get it together.

They want to see me?
But they don't want to see me smiling.
They want to bring their storms to my peaceful islands;

Through all the trials…And…You know…
Disruptions they cause –
To camouflage their flaws – I pause.
    Surprised by nothing; amazing to all…
Expecting nothing less but another test.
I'm cool with it.

    But don't test my cool with it!
They hate me for the same reasons they love me.
    They don't want to have to face their selves…
Yet…So they choose to be ugly.
    Who else but me? Am I the subject of trust?
When for my success they covet and lust?
I thing of it…You must –
    Not – flatter yourself.
Don't badger or batter yourself
    Trying to keep me down, Clown?
'Cuz you don't matter?
    Your help? Was never requested.
And Damn what you suggested!
Can you just respect it?
    You're full of B.S.! I can't detect it?
Yet, once I suspect it, I change from what was first reflected –
    Along with all the false images you
Displayed, portrayed, and projected – We become disconnected;
    Disassociated for a good purpose.
How about all you clowns just get together?
I would love to see a good circus.
    I just get so nervous when there's a surplus
Of brainless individuals operating with short circuits.
Am I cool with it?

    My friends want to burn me; They want to cheat me.
My enemies want to learn me so they can defeat me –
So they can delete me – From existence;

Murder me with deceit and shorten the distance –
I must travel to where destiny will meet me:
Where fate must complete me.
　　But I'm not com-plete-ly exhausted!
You snakes are beneath me!
　　As I am dis-crete-ly exalted – In your minds –
Where I am King of your little thoughts.
I can dig it – I'm cool with it.

　　I'm in school with it –
Teaching you what you don't want to know about me.
Yall can't start the show without me!
　　I'm so far ahead of yall…I'm lonely!
I feel strongly – For my safety!
　　Jealousy, envy, and rage wants to just taste me!
Break me!
　　Eat me alive; swallow me whole!
Patience throttles my soul.
　　From half empty to half full are the bottles I hold;
I never follow – I stroll –
　　As a leader – I set my pace – I'm not a speeder.
Quick to go nowhere fast…on an empty tank with no spare gas.
　　Where's the wisdom in that?
Release your mind from their poisons…in fact,,,
　　I look, listen, study, learn, analyze, then act.
Now who can distract? - My focus?
　　I'm fixed upon the mark of the prize.
I'm out of the dark with wide, open eyes.
　　I Am the Truth!
That causes your lies to be broken down to size.
　　I notice my kinfolk in disguise.
　　I wave like, "Hi Guys!"
'Cuz you know what? I'm cool with it.

　　You wanna know why nothing can stop me?

Because I accept it, don't reject it and surrender it to worry.
    They hurry! – To be just in time
To see my fall and demise. Because they want me buried.
    But I'm called to rise –
Out of the mouth of the grave –
Out of the mouth of the wise.
    I turn 'good-byes' into 'hellos'
And 'hellos' into 'good-byes'.
    Now you think about that!
That's a life-jacket of knowledge.
And you'll sink without that!
I'm cool with it.

    They don't know what to do with it.
They want to know what it is about me that got me swinging;
    Still fighting; still singing;
Still writin' song after song – All day and all night long…
About my life.
    They want to know what it is about me…
That keeps me climbing; rhyming with reason;
    Reaching, teaching, dreaming, speaking, hoping, seeking –
To be someone better…In some place better than this.

    I want to know what it is about me –
And whatever it is has always been –
    And always will be…
Hey…I'm cool with it!

WHAT CAN I SAY?

Things happen; situations occur.
Sometimes the contents in my pot are too thick to stir.
Somehow time and distance has always stood between us.
There's always conflict and battles in one of life's arenas.
But…*What can I say?*

I don't remember all that happened;
I don't know what's going to happen next.
How can I look forward to any thing?
When all consciousness of hope is vexed?
Your love for me has stretched.
As far as love can stretch.
It's like I asked you to throw me a curve ball –
When I knew I couldn't catch.
But, *what can I say?*

I never wanted to worry you.
With all the things in life that were designed to worry me.
Loving you was one thing I was sure I would do.
Until the day this world would bury me.
Sure, I've got a story –
But no one can tell it but me.
Everyone thinks that they know me.
But they're as wrong can be.
If I'm so easy to figure out, why am I so hard to fix?
Why does my heart crumble like sticks?
Why's my head built of bricks?
But you love me and…*What can I say?*

Do you think I really want to use you?
Abuse you?
Confuse you?

No! I refuse to!
There were times I tried to be funny. But it never amused you.
 You've said hurtful things to me.
And in my heart I excused you.
But what more can I say?

 If I apologize for all the bad I've done,
I'd have to apologize for all the good.
 You can't have one without the other.
And I wouldn't change one thing if I could.
 Because if I changed one thing, I'd have to change it all.
Who would change their first tooth or the first day they crawled.
 No one ever had to tell me that you were praying for me.
For some reason or another – I just knew it.
 You could have gave up. But you didn't do it.
You've been a terrific mother. I just blew it.
But, *what can I say?*

 What I *can* tell you is how grateful I am for you.
There is so, so much that I truly thank you for.
 I'm fortunate and blessed – To still have a mother.
This is that moment where I want to thank you more.
 You probably think I don't appreciate you.
Because when it comes to showing you, I'm not too consistent.
 Yet, I know when I have no one else, I'll always have you.
It's just that due to circumstances, I'm forced to be distant.
But, *what can I say?*

 In time, maybe I'll be as strong as you.
For now, I have yet to acquire your strengths;
 See what you've seen; go where you've been.
I have yet to travel such lengths.
 I just want us to be able to understand each other;
Be able to communicate.
 I want to be able to spend some quality time

With you again – Before it's too late.
　　You're my mother and I still need you –
Just as I've always have.
　　I know you miss me hanging out all night with you.
And making you laugh.
　　You always have – And always will –
Mean everything to me in every possible way.
　　I wanted to tell you this…if nothing else:
To me…EVERYDAY is my Mother's day!
Now what else can I say?

LIFE IS A RACE

Life is a race –
It is better to drive to complete.
Rather than strive to compete.
   Life is a unique race –
Not ran on a track. And not ran for competition.
The ribbon at the finish line scratches the mark –
Where destiny is perfected.
   Life is a race –
The crown and trophy is not awarded to the strongest;
Not even the fastest warrants a handshake. The strongest man
Never had his single; most strongest *weakness* challenged. He
never went through the things I went through – like – muscle
pains or being out of breath when exhaustion swelled my lungs or
the fog got too thick to breathe; too poisonous to swallow. The
fastest man never slowed down…to take a good look at life…
Is a race.

   Life was a non-steady pace for him – On your marks? –
Get ready! – Chase! – What?

   One look was one glance away; One glance looked behind;
One peak couldn't. He was afraid of what he would have faced and
become confronted with.. Haste makes waste swiftly and is the
ancient enemy of PATIENCE. Therefore, the fastest one is
more vulnerable…to slips, falls, aches, and breaks.

   Life is a race –
The strongest doesn't always go the longest. Sometimes the
distance is too distant; The farthest is too far; the fast doesn't
always last. No-thing exists! Such as: Warming up and
practicing for this – Life…Is a race.

Is it not why the prize medal in this race is given to he who perseveres? And endures until the race is over? Until completion is achieved? With master-minded achievement? This one: Disciplined and trained – suffered and never gave up: Humble; Sensitive pride subdued – Leaped; stretched over every hurdle – full-stride; DETERMINED; FOCUSED; 'Can't stop now!' attitude. The thought of a short-cut is cut short – For him.

Life was a hell of a race – Through Hell!

It wasn't symbols on the stopwatch that symbolized what measured the runner's determination. Nor that weighed the heart. It wasn't the number of steps he took from beginning to end. Was it the sweat and perspiration of exertion? Or was it the **GOD-FLAVORED** salt of will and drive? It wasn't the cheers or boos from the crowd and spectators that determined or influenced his fate. It was the screams and squeals of his **hope!**
Of his **Belief!**
Of his **Devotion!**
Of his **Confidence!**
That reminded him with every lap:

Life is a race –
And why he raced – Only to stay in front of his self –
And keep that lead.
This one sometimes walked.

IF I COULD
HAVE IT ALL BACK

If I could have it all back:
Just the chance to love you again…
If I could have it all back…This time…
I'd make sure it never ends.

If I could have it all back…
I sure as hell wouldn't be going through this!
If I could have it all back…
I'd make up for every kiss I missed.

I don't want to go back to the way it was.
I just want to go to when it was about to get better.
If I could have it all back…
This time…we would be forever together.

If I could have it all back…
I would listen more to understand more.
If I could have it all back…
We would take more long walks;
Talk while I held your hand more.

If I could have it all back…
I would give it all up again.
I would let nothing tear us up or break us down…
After we build 'us' back up again.

If I could have it all back…
I would change it all around.
I would appreciate when you said you loved me –
And cherished the ground I walked on…
If I could have it all back.

I'd perish if I couldn't have it all back.
This time…I'd hang in there and hang around like a wall plaque;
Stick by your side like a thumb tack.

If I could have it all back…I know I wouldn't share it.
I'd selfishly keep you to myself – Believe me – I'd have to.
I'd have to have your smile again;
I'd have to have your beauty and your grin;

I'd have your heart while mine spins;
I'd have to have you and us as friends.

I'd give all this up…if…
I could have it all back.

MOMMY PLEASE!

Mommy, please don't pour another glass!
I'm having so much trouble in school. And I might not pass.

Mommy, please don't spend your whole check…
On that powdery stuff with those crystal-like specks.

Mommy, please fry us a hamburger patty.
And will I ever get the chance to meet my Daddy?

Mommy, instead of using candles, can we please…
Pay the light bill?
Can we please…buy a heater?
To take away the night chill?

Mommy, please don't swallow anymore of those white pills!
Who is that man, Mommy? Do I have to drink that Nyquil?

Mommy, are you his girlfriend?
Is that what girlfriends are supposed to do?
Since he touches me – Like he touches you –
Mommy, am I his girlfriend too?

Mommy, why can't we bond and connect?
Why don't any of your boyfriends give you respect?

I love you with all my heart! You're so special and sacred!
Mommy, please put on some clothes! Don't go outside half naked!

Don't you know you represent me? And everything I am?
Damn!
Sorry, I'll watch my mouth in your house…
Yes Mommy…I mean yes, Ma'am.

Mommy, please don't hit me again!
My face is all swollen.
Mommy, why did you sell my t.v.?
And tell me that it was stolen?

Mommy, you're changing.
And it gets worse with every segment.
Mommy, Please! Not again!
Don't tell me you're pregnant.

I don't know if it was true.
But I was recently reading…
That the baby is in danger and not healthy…
When you're constantly bleeding.

Mommy, please don't let him beat you again.
Last time , he left fractured bones and broken skin.

Mommy, please don't let him call you a bitch!
I meant, "WITCH!" – Mommy please put down that switch!

It's like my life has been cursed – Woe!
My spirit is so vexed.
And Mommy, what's worse is…
Now, I too enjoy being sexed.

You just wouldn't love me when I asked.
So I found love in the streets.
I'm no longer lonely and afraid…
When I'm naked and in the sheets.

I found happiness in large beds:
Sometimes…three men at a time.
My brother sells me quality dope –
Yes, your son is now, deep into crime.

But something is still missing.
Mommy, I just don't know what to do.
My brother's been murdered over drugs.
And all I have now is you!

* * * * * * * * * * * * * * * * *

Mommy, please eat something for me!
You've lost so much weight.
And please take your medication.
And stop saying that it's too late.

It cut me so deep. And all I could say was, "Why me?"
When the doctors said you were positive for H.I.V.

You're still young and so sweet;
So full of life; filled with charm.
Mommy, please wake up!
And take that silly needle out of your arm!

Mommy, please don't die yet!
They say you're brain-dead; comatose.
But I don't believe them!
It was just a stupid, little overdose!

* * * * * * * * * * * * * * * *

**Well, it's fifteen years later. I'm a college grad; happily
married.**
Mommy, please open your eyes!
This is your grandchild I carried.

I named her after you. She kind of scared us for a while.
But she made it! And Mommy, look. She even has your smile.

I love you so much! I miss you in my life!
Mommy, how could you forget to teach me…
How to be a mother and a wife?

Mommy, please tell me you love me.
I don't know how many times I've asked it.
    For now, I'll just place these flowers right next to you –
Here, in your casket...Damn!

    Yes, Ma'am I will watch my mouth at your funeral.

5 GREAT WONDERS

- *(Feel) – 1.}*

I wonder what you feel like:
Body temperature just right?
I wonder what your body feels like pressed up against mine.
I wonder what you feel like from the front and from behind.
I wonder what you feel like on the tips of my fingers;
In the palms of my hands –
When your legs are stretched wide.
And your opening expands.
I wonder what you feel like warm, wet, and ready –
Deep in the center.
I wonder what you feel like outside of those clothes.
Allow my curiosity to slowly enter.
I wonder what you feel like –
Lying right next to me in ecstasy.
Paradise inside of paradise –
Is what I imagine sex would be.
Do you feel cool in the daytime?
Juices on fire in the middle of the night?
Do you feel cool under the sun?
And sweltering hot under the moonlight?
I wonder if you feel like Heaven.
If so, may I penetrate Heaven's gates?
I wonder what it would feel like to find out…
That we were always Soul-Mates.

- *(Sound) – 2. }*

I wonder what you sound like whispering in my ear.
I wonder what you sound like in the dark.
Let's turn off the lights so I can hear.

I wonder what you sound like…
When you're moaning and purring my name.
I wonder what you sound like when I'm breathing hard –
And you're breathing the same.
I wonder what you sound like –
When you, "Ooh," and when you, "Ahh"
I wonder what you'd sound like…
Singing me a live love-song, Ma-Ma›
I wonder what you sound like…
When your juices are splashing;
The walls behind your hot-spot are crashing;
And all the warning lights are flashing.
When you first spoke to me,
You had the sexiest voice I'd ever heard.
I wonder what you'd sound like…
If you had never spoken a word.

-   *(Smell) – 3. }*

I wonder what you smell like:
Your eyes are closed.
And I'm rubbing you down in perfumes and oils.
Your panties are soiled with wet desire.
Your sweet passion boils and boils.
(I bet you smell soooo gooood!)
I wonder what you'd smell like in a champagne bubble bath
Two bottles of baby oil; one thousand rose petals:
One tub; two bodies – you do the math.
How about some pink suds on top of a pink tub –
Filled with pink champale?
I'm willing to gamble my heart on this:
You'd be a pleasant treat and a delight to inhale.
I know of an aroma that I can't wait to smell.
And that's your skin dripping cherry –

Mixed with a Raspberry laurel.
　　Scented candles fragrancing the bedroom;
The scent of you captured in the wind.
　　Hypnotic; intoxicating – Me and you perspirating:
I'm gone, caught up, and captured by the blend.
　　I wonder what you smell like in a bed of strawberries –
As your body discharges its steam.
　　How about I bring the chocolate syrup?
And you bring the whipped cream?
　　I wonder what your hair smells like…
When I'm kissing you on your ears and your neck.
　　You exhale after every peck.
It's taking its toll and its effect.
　　I wonder if you smell like chocolate chip.
Because girl, you gotta cookie with your fannie!
　　I saw it the first time you sat in front of me.
And I want every nook and crannie.

- 　*(Look) – 4. }*

　　I wonder what you look like lying naked on satin sheets.
Forgive me for being weak.
But I've been wondering about this for weeks.
　　I wonder what you look like with your eyes closed –
Dreaming of me.
　　I wonder what you look like …
With your legs forming the capital letter, 'V'.
　　I wonder what you look like wearing nothing…
But a smile and a thong.
　　I've been wondering all day long –
About me giving you this work and piling it on.
(Did I say something wrong?)
　　I wonder what you look like…
When my eyes are closed tight.

We're on a sandy, white beach –
Making love under the moon and star-light.
I wonder what you look like when you're sad –
I need to know.
So I can be the one to always give you that glow.
I was impressed…
By your thighs, your hips, your ass, and your breasts.
I wonder what you look like…
In an all white wedding dress.
I want to know what you look like in the shower –
Let me pull back the curtain.
I'm gonna find out what you look like –
In see-through lingerie.
That's one thing for sure and two things for certain.
I wonder what you look like under the blankets…
Drenched in hot sweat.
I can picture and imagine how glistening wet –
You actually can get.
I wonder what you look like –
Even though I've already stared into your eyes.
I wonder what we look like together:
Forever a part of each other's lives.

- *(Taste)* – **5.** }

I wonder what you taste like –
I'm just dying to see.
My mouth is watering for your good stuff.
May I let my tongue go free?
Great taste; less filling; zero calories; zero grams.
I wonder if you taste like soft, melted marshmallows –
Cooked inside of sweet, candied yams.
I wonder what you taste like…
In warm caramel and hot butterscotch.
Hershey's Kisses with almonds and French vanilla –

Slow down, Mommy – I just wanna watch.
Before we turn it up a notch.
　　I wonder what you taste like…
Slow-cooked in sticky cinnamon.
　　I want to lick you all over…
And taste your adrenalin.
　　I wonder what you taste like above and below the hips.
Relax and prepare for climax as I part your lips.
　　They tell me that temperatures rise –
When you're heading down south.
　　I hunger and thirst for your jewels.
So I'm putting your pearl in my mouth.
　　I wonder what you taste like…
In wild-berry or black-cherry panties.
　　I wonder if you will melt in my mouth – Like warm-milk
chocolate or cotton candy.
　　I'm starving for your delicate pleasure.
I wonder how this craving can be so overpowering.
　　I wonder what your patty-melt tastes like.
If I've got my lips on you…
I wonder if you can handle the devouring.

　　I had to confess that I had been wondering about you.
I'll go crazy if I have to start wondering what it feels like without
you. – Or what the room sounds like without the presence of your
laughter.
　　Do you remember our first time together? And the
morning that came after?
　　You smelled like a fresh rose to my young, virgin nose.
I wondered if you had spilled honey dew melon on your clothes.
　　You would even smile in wonder –
If you knew what I had you doing in my dreams.
　　Just the thought of me stewing; brewing in your creams…
Is the sweetest taste I've ever known…
　　(Just absolutely beautiful!)

REMEMBER…

I remember my days of innocence;
When life was all simple.
I remember growing the first hair on my face…
Like I remember my first pimple.
I remember how I loved to see my mother smile.
And how I thought she was jewel.
I remember oatmeal and cereal in the mornings –
And watching cartoons before heading to school.
I remember the lunchroom highs;
Trading cream-filled pies –
And how pretty girls would make me nervous.
I remember hiding my ties;
Then telling silly lies.
So I wouldn't have to go to Sunday service.
I remember walking home with my buddies saying,
"If you step on a crack , you break your mother's back."
I remember being the 'bad seed' – The 'black sheep' –
But the sharpest needle in the haystack.
I remember the winter's cold –
Like I remember the summer's heat.
I remember the broken glass out on my street…
Crunching under my feet.
I remember neighborhood parks, arcade…
And the time there I spent.
I remember being lonely, being popular,
And how friends came and went.
I remember when playing in mud and splashing in puddles
Was considered to be fun.
I remember chasing the ice-cream truck –
And how he drove so slow, we barely had to run.
I remember going to McDonald's –

And eating happy-meals down to the last crumb.
    I remember my school bus driver,
My kindergarten teacher,
And I remember where I came from.
    I remember dreaming of you.
And that's something I'll never regret.
    Then I remember meeting you; noticed our eye-connect,
And my next thought...I'll never forget.
    I remember thinking, 'I think I'm already in love.'
Oh yes...I remember it well.

I DON'T KNOW

I don't know why I don't know. I don't know what to look for. I don't know what to listen for. I don't know what to live for. I don't know what to die for. I don't know what to ask for. I don't know what to wait for. I don't know what I want. I don't know what I need. I don't know what I love. I don't know what I hate. I don't know what to offer. I don't know what to expect. I don't know what to cherish. I don't know what to regret. I don't know what to remember. I don't know what to forget. I don't know who to run to. I don't know who to walk away from. I don't remember it all. I must have forgotten it all. I don't know if I ever knew. I don't know what to think or learn next. I don't know what to hold on to. I don't know what to let go of. I don't know what it is. I don't know the reason for any of it. I don't know what to listen to. I don't know what to tune out. I don't know what to accept. I don't know what to refuse. I don't know what it means. I don't know why it seems like I should know. I don't know why I don't know. What do I know? But what I do know is what I do know. That's nothing at all. All is nothing in the end. Truly a fading illusion. However, I never said I didn't know anything.

THE LIONS' DEN

    I was thrown into the lion's den for wrongs –
I did not commit.
    Like when Peter denied the Christ:
Those closest to me would soon forget.

    Beasts behaving with harshness;
Breath exhaling each carcass;
    Heirs of the damned darkness –
So damned brutal and so damned heartless.

    The earth became sunken –
Under the pressure of their paws;
    Sharp and razor-like claws;
Mighty and powerful – The vice of their jaws!

    They plotted; stewed in the stench of the rotted –
Threatening with saber-like teeth.
    I couldn't; absolutely wouldn't!
Let them on top…just to lie helplessly underneath.

    Many men will die in a war –
While many others live as the coward.
    I counted many bodies in the lion's den:
Lifeless but had not been devoured.

    I sensed that these hungry animals
Starved for blood that was fresh;
    Flavored with the scent of fear –
Which is the weakness of the flesh.

    Saliva oozed from their tongues
As they thirsted for my sweat:

Tender and palatable between their gums –
Becoming the sum of all my debts.

"Welcome to the lion's den.
Here, only the strongest one wins.
   "Unfortunately, it is now time
That you paid for all of your sins.

   "Your life is over! Give up!
There's no making sweet amends.
   "No one will come to deliver you – Not family.
Where are your friends?"

   I laughed at the lion –
Though he was wild and atrocious.
   He roared and he howled – Far from mild –
But loud and ferocious!

   I continued to smile.
The lion began to speak again.
   He said, *"Do you not realize?*
You are in the lion's den!

   "The world gave up on you. How ill you survive?
"They threw in the towel,
Knowing that you'll never leave here alive!

   "They don't care about you!
And how dare you stand there and laugh!
   "Everyone you trusted deserted you!
And that's not even the half.

   "I'm the King of this jungle!
I'll break you and make you crumble!
   "You will respect my Majesty –
And at once! – Become humble!"

"Have you lost your mind?" I asked.
"Is there someone you think I resemble?
"Is this where I should start running?
"Or should I just shake and tremble?

"Yeah, I'm on an ocean; in a storm;
"In a canoe and without a paddle.
"I straddled this horse with no saddle.
"Because I can fight my own battle.

"When this cage starts to rattle,
I will lose skin to win skin.
"I will strike with Royal Authority –
As <u>Your</u> King in this lion's den.

"I've been hated; envied; attacked –
But conquerors aren't defeated!
"I wear the real crown: On a throne of my own.
I refuse to be defeated.

"I'm not scared of you one bit!
And I hope you've been enlightened.
"How dare you speak to me as if –
I'm supposed to be frightened!"

The lions began to back away.
They smelled my furry as I scowled.
They began to circle me stealthily.
They growled as they prowled.

The lion spoke one, last time: His voice grumpy and rough;
His tone gruff as he said, *"Oh, so you think you're tough?!*
"I could pounce on you at any second –
With such force in my attack!
"I'd clench onto your throat fiercely –
Before you even had time to react!

"We will rip you from limb to limb!
We will tear you apart!
"We will shred you into pieces!
We will feast on that brave, little heart!

"You are in the lion's den!
Didn't you hear me say that before?
"And here, in the lion's den,
Only death is in store and life no more.

"You almost convinced me there –
With your whining exasperations.
"Now, I will convince you –
With some defining lacerations!"

"Now hold on there Tiger!
You might wanna turn on some light."

"Why?" He asked.
"Don't get scared now! It's time to fight!"

"Well, I question the ability of your sight.
That's a lot of gall for even you to haul.
"What makes you think I'm so easy to maul?
I'm afraid the truth is: I'm not afraid of you at all."

"In the lion's den, everyone's afraid!
Who doesn't know that we're mean and cruel?
"I think you're either one hell of a liar…
Or one hell of a fool!

"With just one of my paws,
I'll squash you like a fly!
"Cocky? – You dare to mock me?
Now you must die! Say, 'Good-bye'!"

They crouched – But courageously – So did I.
Then they refrained.
   We remained – Poised and restrained –
Silenced and sustained – Then I explained:

"You see, I know that you're a lion.
And I am well aware of what lion's do.
   "But what <u>you've</u> not noticed or realized is that
Boo!...I am a lion too!"

   "I won't succumb to a predator.
I too, will hunt and chase.
   "Now that the sun is rising, Mr. Lion,
Take a good look at my face"

   His eyebrows were raised.
His smirk became a frown.
   They snarled at the words I'd just spoken.
But the den of lions backed down.

   A new day was dawning –
AS this new revelation was now spawning.
   The haughty lion was now nervous;
Apologetic and now fawning.

   "Why didn't you just say so, my friend?
Of course we really wouldn't have eaten you.
   "Something about you had told us:
We really couldn't have beaten you.

   "We were just sort of testing you –
You know…to see if you were brave.
   "I didn't really mean those nasty things I said.
This is not how we usually behave."

   It was at that point – I realized –
Where in my life I stood –

Mentally – No longer in the lion's den:
The bad was all for my good.

I stared at my antagonists –
As he riddled off his excuse.
I knew he had once intended…
inflicting upon me grave abuse.

I was unscathed physically –
But so emotionally scarred;
Terribly; so mentally exhausted –
As if we had – in fact – sparred.

In time, I'll forgive my betrayers.
I'm sorry. But only God knows when.
And to all those who abandoned me – To struggle:
Behold! – I escaped the lion's den!
I've got nothing but love for you all!

Writer's Commentary:

You may not want to believe that the game's true –
Until this part of the game comes to life and claims you.
I can't count all the deserts, storms, and lion's dens
I came through.
Just know that somewhere on the list of life's adversity –
Bears your name too!

P.T.G.

…NOT LIKE YOU SHOULD

You don't believe in the boogie-man?
But you're afraid of the dark?
You can't swim in deep waters?
But you're in love with a shark?

The truth is: I left you to spend more time –
With a prison guard.
I always loved multiplication and addition.
But Baby, division's hard!

I would change it all around.
I would come back if I could –
Even though you don't have my back…
At least, not like you should.

You knew I was a hustler.
You were well aware of my affairs.
Born in a jungle of gorillas;
Wild-Life raised – In a forest with bears.

I had to get it ; you was down with it –
For the love of the money;
To the bitter from sweet honey.
And now you sho'll is actin' funny!

I took the burns from the fire.
I swung the axe; chopped the wood.
Now you don't even write me…
At least…Not like you should.

Are you moving on with your life?
Should I say my 'Good-byes'?

Should I be surprised?
I expected all of this from all of my guys.

Am I doing this time?
Because it seems like this time is doing you.
Girl, without you by my side –
What the hell am I supposed to do?

I'll break the law to survive.
Did we not have this understood?
But now, you choose not to communicate…
At least…not like you should.

I love you! I really miss you!
And this is killing me inside.
To see you unstrap your seatbelt –
And jump out of this ride.

I now feel alone in this car. Destination unknown!
I've gotta write you; gotta see you;
Gotta hear your voice on the phone.

To say that you've never been there?
That's not what I mean.
But don't change when the leaves turn brown –
And the grass is no longer green.

I need you here when it's cold;
Not just here when it's warm.
Don't show up at the end of the rainbow –
If you weren't here in the storm.

Now we're apart –
Perhaps things are definitely not the same.
It's breaking my aching heart!
Darling, you need to step up your game.

You don't tell me you love me...
At least...not like you should.
But I already know you do.
So, it's truly all to the good.

Hold me down!

JUST THINKING

I was just thinking about something –
Where could I find the word, expression, or phrase?
How could I count the days?
Or measure the ways?

How could I number the memories? They're quite a few.
How could I total the feelings that I feel for you?

If I balanced the scales of our friendship,
What would it equal to?
How could I sum up all that we've been through?

The answer is: Baby, I most certainly couldn't.
And if you asked me to try…Honestly?…I wouldn't.

I can only be grateful for the bond we share.
We are a rare pair.
But I'm blessed because you've always been there.

[Just Thinking About You!]

TO WHOEVER'S LISTENING

Things just ain't the same no more.
My patience has been rocked from its foundation to its core.
These waves have carried me too far from the shore.
And I can't help but to imagine what more life has in store.
Why does everyone I know want to hurt me for?
Why did they tempt a lion? Just to hear him roar?
I've fallen in love with Beauty. And she's a whore.
Why have I become something ugliness won't ignore?
I love the things I hated.
And the things I loved, I abhor
I never knew I had a heart –
Until it tore.
I never knew I was asleep to the game –
Until I heard me snore.
Sometimes life is such a bore.
And other times, living it is such a chore.
But when I think of walking out of that door,
I tell myself that it's more to life for me to explore.
I'm constantly losing and time is keeping the score.
So far, there was a lot more pains than smiles I wore.
My emotions are like shattered glass on a marble floor.
And at the end of this game, things will never be the same…
NO MORE!

WHEN YOU ENTERED MY DREAMS

When you entered my dreams, My rest became peaceful. When you entered my life, my dreams came alive. Before you entered my atmosphere, my world was void and unknown. Now I have a broader conception and a wider projection of a beautiful dream.

When you entered my dreams,
My empty and destitute soul began to swell with the contents of your lovely essence. My dreams were uninhabited. Then, you entered. The darkness that I once saw when I closed my eyes has vacated and completely vanished. Now when I open them I'm engulfed with total, illuminated fantasies of you.

Dreaming of you has become my ultimate desire; my ultimate reality. To study you is to learn you. This is my homework assignment and trivial pursuit. Connections with who you are is my most valued project.

When you entered my dreams, my everything changed. I don't sleep like I used to. When awake, I'm not the same. Am I conscious or incoherent? Am I aware or delusional? Do I know what I know? What matters is what I feel. What's real is what I first saw in my heart…when you entered my dreams.

P.S. When you entered my dreams, your eyes were closed. That's when I supposed that you were dreaming of me.

LOVE IS LIKE A SYMPHONY

Two loves as one should be like a symphony: The most gorgeous, extraordinary, and interesting qualities about symphonies are that they're all comprised of strong notes by strong instruments that, together, make strong chords. They involve precious strings that are being stretched to their limitations; that are delicately stroked – provoking and inducing the most audible seduction on the ears.

Winds instruments that are bringing forth sounds of love by the breathing; the all powerful exhaling of life into them; bells and symbols representing the intensity of amazement, impulsiveness, adventure, and wonder as well as being symbolic to the escalating pulsation of excitement and joy.

There are no drums; no barbaric sticks beating and banging a conclusive concussion into the percussions – No kicking the bass – Just all instrumental and sophisticated melody.

Harmony: Thick and sweet like honey – The kind that makes you wake up at sunrise and say, "Good morning, Honey!" All the while, the two of you smile at how two loves musically became 'one' like a symphony of love.

I'M ALMOST SURE OF IT

Happiness and security comes with peace and success. You also have to increase hope and belief. You have to trust yourself to make the right decisions about people and occurrences.

Fear has no place in happiness and security. Fear is the absolute faith and positive belief that failure and negativity will manifest in the crop of every decision we make.

Trials teach us how to travail and prevail. Tribulations teach us how to triumph and celebrate our over comings instead of mourning our shortcomings.

Pain teaches us how to appreciate and enjoy peace and pleasure. Loss teaches us how to cherish and preserve that which is precious and valuable. Absence makes presence more desirable.

Regrets are just bad memories of those horrible mistakes we've made, can't change and haven't gotten over.

Indecision is the self-conscious self that is unconscious to the 'true' self and doesn't believe who you are and what you can do.

Arrogance is the crack in the step that gives and makes the climber fall just when he thought he'd reached the top.

But confidence and humility is the wisdom of understanding the blessing to have achieved the 'little' and the awareness of the long journey of experiences and lessons that lie ahead and lead to further and greater achievements.

Happiness and security is the result of mastering and conquering the misery and insecurity of your most fortified opponent: You! As a matter of fact – I'm almost sure of it!

LETTING YOU BACK INTO MY LIFE

I keep letting you back into my life. But no more!
You'll just continue to do the same disrespectful things as before.
You keep pretending like you love me –
And I just keep loving you to the core.
But you can't come back into my life.
I won't let you back through that door.
It's funny how you remind me of someone I once knew.
They too hurt me, lied to me, and betrayed me like you do.

And I keep letting you back into my life.
Shame on me! Blame's on me!
How could I've mistakenly let you –
Run that game on me?
Could I live without you and forget?
You'd better believe it! Because Baby, I sho' could!
When we touched, it felt sooooo googood!
But the truth is: You're sorry, mentally 'touched', and no good!
You throw bad wood on a fire –
That I can't stop from burning.
But if every experience is educational –
You can't knock me for learning.
It's like I can't stop this yearning for your touch.
And your embrace.
But you don't deserve me –
So, in my life, you have no place.

I keep letting you back in my life.
I must have very bad taste.
How could I choose someone like you?
I never again want to see your face.
You pushed me away.
Well, it was more like 'shoved'.

I asked myself why.
It was because you never wanted to be loved.
    I was your blessing from above;
The one blessing you never counted.
    I begged you to come down off of your high horse –
But you never dismounted.

    I'm closing the door to my life;
There's no more letting you back in.
    No more bending over backwards;
Doing back-flips and back-bends.
    What we have as of now's a has-been:
Bad blood; bad skin: Scraps for the trash bin.
    When we first met, you truly had class then.
Now you're a bad taste in my mouth: Indigestion –
I need an aspirin!
    Now it's all over! No more chances; slow dances;
No more strife.
    Because this time…
I won't be letting you back into my life.

MY DILEMMA

Writer's Commentary: I was disturbed by my dilemma and its vexatious effect which laid heavily upon my haunted spirit. I was impeccably challenged with what to make of it: To share the wealth of my knowledge pertaining to its existing elements and the peril which they contain per diem. There is no place in all the universe which is safe and non-dangerous. But there is only; only one individual, universal place which is pure in its conscience and all of its innocence: The closest place to true purity and what is purely Godly. That place is in the imagination of a child. (Far from the machinations of mankind). Protect them. Don't hurt them. For in the pulse of my uncouth imagination was contrived this dilemma...My Dilemma!

There is forbidden fruit on the tree of life –
There is abortion in the womb –
There's the Boogie-man under the bed –
There is glass on the playground –
There is salt in the wound –
There are drugs in the schools –
There is betrayal in the blood –
There are hell-raising devils in the heavens –
Some people find heaven in hell –
There are fire-breathing angels in hell –
There is hell on earth –
There are serpents in the garden –
There are poisonous seeds in the apple –
There is healing in the weeds –

There is death in life –
There is no life in death –
There is true life after true death.

There is a resurrecting in the decomposing –
Disappointments and fears are in the days –
There's nightmares at the dawns of the mornings –
There is pain in love –
There is great love for great pain –
There are lies in the promises –
There are truths in disappointments –
There are test mice in the labyrinths and mazes of life –
There are rats that will have you trapped in a life of mazes –

There is darkness in the wilderness –
There is wickedness in wishing upon the stars –
There are rats in the alleys too –
There are fleas on the dog –
There are knots and kinks in the ropes and strings of success –
There are risks in achievements –
There are crabs on the beach –
Now they are in the bucket –Now they are on my heels –

There are crows in the corn fields –
And devoured cobs next to the sugar cane –
There are skeletons in the closet –
There are skeletons who want to pick bones with me –
There are ghosts in the past –
There is a past that chases one away from his future –
There are monsters present in my presence –
There are demons waiting for me in my future –

There are hurricanes in the summers –
There are blizzards in the winters –
The winters are too hot –
The spring and summer is too cold –
There's the hail in the rain –
There's hell in the drops –
There's no sign of the morning dew –

There is famine on the farms –
There is homelessness in the United States –
There is war where there was peace –
There are thorns on the rose stems –
The rose sometimes grows in darkness –
There is beauty in the thorns but ugliness in the petals –

There is a fly in the manure –
Now the fly is in the soup –

There are spiders under the rocks –
There are roaches in the projects; living in my cereal box –
There are mosquitoes in the tents –
There are red ants in the picnic baskets –
There is a hidden meaning for the word, 'picnic' –

There is thunder and lightning in the driest clouds –
There is dry land under the oceans and seas –
There is drowning in the sand –
There is virus and disease in the air –
(Disease is mad in the cow) –
There is mold on the bread –
There is high blood pressure in the pig –
There are vultures, bats, and hawks in the skies –
There are eyes on the eagles and eagle in the eyes –
There is pollen in the breeze –
There are bees in the honey and bears in the hives –

There is cancer in the breast –
There is diabetes in the apple pie –
There are liquor stores in the Asiatic communities –
(They stay open longer than community centers) –
Longer than the doors to wisdom and the knowledge of self –

There are guns in the fifth grade lockers –
There is unprotected sex in adolescence –

There are racial slurs at recess –
There is traitorism in the beloved kiss –
There is joy in misery –
There is beautiful sadness in horrible happiness –

There are crocodiles in the marshes –
There are alligators in the swamps –
There are sharks in the waters –
There are scorpions in the sands of the deserts –
There are snakes in the bushes –
There are snakes in the grass –
There are snakes in love, friendships, and associations –
There are wolves in the mountains –
There are foxes in the valleys –
There are bears in the caves –
There are gorillas in the forests –
There are lions in the jungles –
There are two worst adversaries…
Who are two of the greatest friends –
There is companionship in the congregation of my enemies –
There are fathers in the beds of daughters –
There are mothers' strangled bodies in the lakes –

There's divorce in the fake sanctity of European marriage -
There are stray bullets at three year olds' birthday parties –
There is child molestation in the sacraments of priesthood –
There are pedophiles at Disney World –
There's terrorism and suicide bombing in feigned religious faith –
There is a star in the east –
There is blood in the west –
There is beauty in the beast –
There is a curse in being blessed –

There is deception and brainwashing in…
Education and politics –
There is greed and theft in economics –

There is slavery and prejudice in corporate business
And social development –
There is discrimination and sexual harassment
In the office place –
There is poor judgment and poor justice
In the poor jury and poor judicial system for the poor –
There are contradictions in the oath, 'To serve and protect' –
There is captivity in the constitution –
There is a crime in being denationalized and labeled as, 'black' –
There is corruption in the police department –
There are more railroads in the courtrooms
Than on tracks all across the countries –
There is violence and recidivism in the prison industry –
There is genocide and depravity in the richness of
Afrika and America –
There is a joke in being called, 'African-American'. –
(But it's not funny!)

　　There is trickery and treachery in the –
United States Constitution –
There are signs in the symbols and symbols in the signs –
There are slaves, hostages, and prisoners in the land of the free –
There are conniving cowards in the home of the brave –
There is two-fifths missing from three-fifths of a man –
There's been Nationality and Divine creed…
Removed from the spirit, body, and soul of the Afrikan man –

　　There is poverty…
Within the boundaries of the most prosperous
And wealthiest super-power in the world –

　　There are foreign drugs on America's domestic streets –
(Mostly among American-born, foreign 'minorities'.) –
'I-Am-Race' is found in the word, 'America'. –
There is hatred in families and kindred. -

There is misguidance, misrepresentation, as well as –
Inadequate, incompetent, and inappropriate leadership –
In the, (so-called), African-American societies –
There is abandonment in trial and tribulation –
There are graves in the cemeteries –
There is a shallow grave that holds Hiram Abiff -
Finally…
There are worms in the grave

<u>2nd Commentary</u> - When I learned myself, studied my way of thinking, and evaluated my self-ability to analyze and reason using logic, ethics, educated intelligence, and moral principle; When I considered my <u>Dilemma</u> – giving recognition and acknowledgement to my entanglement in the web of my imbroglio of inner and deep-seated curiosities which slowly – in time – deteriorates and disempowers me; when I pondered over the ill-will and atrocity of my <u>Dilemma</u> which entails and promises no change leading towards solution thus far, I came to the conclusion that I would rather suffer close encounters with all of these situations and their attachments – all at once – than wake up, (just one time), in the scorn of a woman or in the heart of mankind…Now that's my <u>Dilemma!</u>

THE PRINCIPLE OF UNITY

This is my understanding of unity and all its principles.
Unity is faith in the omnipresent, omnipotent, and invincible.
The most High – He and I – All-Powerful –
And incomprehensible;
Most Gracious – even to the unwise and non-sensible.

This my creativity:
To be an inspiration to the creativity of man –
In my attempts to always do as much as I can –
In any way that I can.
It is my purpose to build and construct –
In the community of my people: (In communion with my people).
To develop and restore greatness –
As we struggle faithfully together as equals.
It is my business to make business – accessible –
To bring economics to the storefront of our community;
To share in all its work, worth, and wealth –
And pursue organization and unity.
I understand the importance of healthy relationships –
With my sisters and brothers.
I understand our responsibility –
To uplift one another.
I am a voice and a pillar;
The definition of strength in my society.
With self-determination…
We will prosper triumphantly and not quietly!

We must strive for pure harmony.
And capitalize on every fortunate opportunity.
As a family and world Asiatic community –
With principled togetherness and unity!

TRUST

Trust is not easy to come by.
To trust is hard to do though some try.
Trust is hard to find when searched for.
With love and respect – Trust is worth more.
Trust promotes no deceit or lies.
It won't betray, cheat, or despise.
It's honest, truthful; it bonds; it ties:
Never phony, fake, or sneaky; in disguise.
It never sees through jealous eyes.
Know who to and who not to trust and be wise.
Trust is not shady or sheisty.
It is earned when worked for – It is pricey.
Trust believes until the truth comes out.
Strong, solid: Beyond a reasonable doubt.
It won't give up or act flaky.
It won't walk out when facts look shaky.
Trust joins and never separates.
It's the spice of love like pepper flakes.
If I have pure trust in my heart –
I have no worries when we're apart.
If I can trust you through and through –
I know my feelings are safe with you.
If I can trust you until the end –
Only then – Can I call you a friend.
If we don't have trust to wean us through –
We don't have nothing between us two.

YOU'LL BE LOYAL

If you can first be loyal to yourself, your word, and your promises, then and only then can you be loyal to another's heart; to another's faith in you and to another's belief that you will be loyal under the kind of weight and pressure of weakness that can shatter strength and loyalty in pieces.

If you can be loyal to your instincts, insights, and intuitions, only then can you be loyal to our secrets, our discretions, and our dreams. You'll be loyal to the expectations that we share for life. You'll be loyal to the locks that secure our universe and the doors to our worlds.

If you can be loyal in little things, you can be trusted with great things in greater places. You'll be loyal to our bond and the commitment of our worlds together.

If you can be loyal to me while I'm on the bottom, I'll be loyal to you when I make it back on top.

CAN ANYBODY HEAR ME?

Tear-stained ashes; Burning soul of guilt;
Crumbled emotionalism – Humbled and motionless is my state –
Such as I am…
No longer such as I was:

Reflections of worry in every spectrum of light –
Penetrating fallen eyelids and burglarizing my unsettled soul.
Weariness is the marrow in my bones.
Can anybody hear me?

I am alone –
Thoughts shaped by utter blackness – Blackness?
As in B.L.A.C.K.?
Darkness blankets my joy.
Paintings of confusion framed in a broken heart.
Cluttered pieces breaking more and more and more and more –
Scattered images of this broken vessel.

Distorted.

Smiles abandon me.
Happiness left me to die.
Horrible sounds of scampering gallops:
Those of fleeing companions.
And friends.
Rapidly growing further in the distance.

Sight blurred; Dear obstructed vision:
Be thou far from me.
Where did everyone go?

I'm neither here nor there –
But separated from life – Every now, here, there.
This life which art masked and unidentifiable.

Is anyone listening?

I am alone.
Everything left; No thing is left.
But what is this? – My love has returned to me like a dove…
After the flood…
After is when?
Undeniable rejection.
Wrapped in the arms of this storm..

Exhausted.
Eyeing for its eye – to look upon me.

Escaped air from punctured lungs.

Alarms whistle – As panic is on a hunt for my serenity.
Madness sniffs me out like a deranged stalker.
Hatred is on my trail and picking up my scent.

Is anyone there?
I am alone.
Where is alone?

Puddles of sweat encompasses my palms.
Nausea umbrellas my hunger pangs.

Starless skies –
With no hope of a rising sun.
The moon can't find its glow.

My faith: Like shards of broken glass;
Shattered pieces of sharp and piercing memories.
Regrets like dagger-shaped and frozen icepicks…
Cutting away at my solace and contentment.

Smiles for the better –
Only to be replaced by frowns for the worse.

Does anyone understand me?
I am alone.
Hollowness and emptiness overwhelm me.
All that is absent to no longer return.

Unstrained; untamed lines…running loose and wild.
Unleashed and un-censored hatred.
Scratching at the hard-wood floors of my sanity.

Unlimited broken promises – In pursuit of my desires –
And anxious anticipations.

Mountains of disappointments…
Towering over valleys of frivolous expectations.
My sight: So, so distorted and distracted by optical illusions.
I'm seeing things.
I can't see a thing.

Can anybody hear me?
Who am I talking to?

Sweat-soaked sheets of paranoia –
In the coldness of the night.

The moon is getting carried away.
The moon's carried away and once again…
Darkness covers the faces of the deepest of my interpretations.

Divisions of dimensions –
Dimensions of divisions.

What is this dementia?
Haunted by delusional, phantomous apparitions.
My closest companion is a ghost.
Hope murdered my criminalistic nightmares.
Nightmares, too relentless, murdered my hope.

Physically assaulted by migraines;
Paralyzed by betrayal.
Brutalized –
By the pounding of my own erratic pulse.

So unrealistic.
Pillow cases saturated by liquid salt.

Cold!
Freezing blood clogging my arteries.
The hot, crimson liquid of burning copper…
Brewing in every white and red cell.

Can anybody hear me?
My own blood bears its fangs unremittingly.
The sweat of my pores deceive me.

My body quivers:
Black cave of a world.

So chilling life is.
Days like electrocuting bolts of lightning:
Spiraling down to strike this tree.
My adam's apple flirts with the blade of the axe.
The sword has asked for my head.
The hammer dreams of my skull:
Crashing against the bottoms of this…helpless temple.

Lost boundaries; undiscovered.
Dispersed forever.

Whose creation?

Can anybody hear me?

My faith and optimism has teamed up –
And declared war against me.

Stillness keeps moving.
And now, time has drawn its weapon.

Another time racing.
Seconds like armed horsemen.
Minutes like chariots.
The hours too powerful to number.

Special movements - like suicidal soldiers –
Marching to be slaughtered in the battle.
Cornered.
Caged.
Solitaire confinement.

Heart beating with the beat of revenge.
Pulse eager to avenge the beating it suffers.

Lungs burning with scorn.

Nostrils melting from spite – Nose bleed!
Animalistic instincts: Cravings of the beast.
Unpredictably dangerous.
Vitals unstable.

This testament: A declaration of defenselessness.
Contradictory or usual nature?
Sorrowful.
So uncharacteristic: Casually abnormal.

Changing seasons.
Again – seasons change…
Beyond and foreign to familiar conditions.

Survival: Undetermined.

Who have I become? But that fallen tree?
Broken branches – stretched out across the forest's basement.
Do I make noise? Did sound travel?

Dispatching rescue.
Do you read me?
Or am I over and out?
No emergency lights?
No flares?
No hounds to sniff me out and find me?

No one can hear me.
I am alone.
Unjustifiable silence.

UNBREAKABLE

Still unbreakable! – Still un-brake-able!
Drive: Untraceable!
Glass – But not see-through; sharp but un-shattered.
    Knocked down –
But still standing as if the punches had never mattered.
    Their strength is mere weakness –
My weakness is pure strength..
    Pound for pound; round for round –
From the first bell to ten rounds past the tenth.

    The things that they're running into –
Are the things that I'm calmly walking away from.
    I'm lonely because I'm ten steps ahead of those bums;
A ten foot pole away from being plumb-dumb.

    When I complain –
Everything negative seen and unseen – I seem to attract.
    All the while, I smile – To make the world walk a mile –
To take two steps back.
    Patience in tact –
React with quick wit.
    Analyze and observe before I act;
Steer clear of the sucka-shit!
    Unshakeable; Unmistakably unbreakable!
Of this thing, I'm certain and for sure.
    You can't make me drown – You can't take me down!
I will always persevere and endure.
    You still trying to break me, clowns?
Searching my face for frowns?
Amazed that I'm alive with so many snakes around?
    I can't forsake my ground…

No matter the heartaches – I'm bound…
To melt away the blizzard and every snowflake that's found.

Turn snow into water - Turn water into storms.
Make it flood; Pour dirt over mud –
And watch the whole earth re-form.

I'm re-created and re-born:
Broke through the rain and the water bag.
All of the pain that I *thought* I had –
Ain't half of the pain that I ought of had.
Once again – I win – With class and style;
Another million dollar smile –
Survival and success on speed-dial.
Flowing as coolly and as smoothly –
As the currents in the Nile.
Profile unreadable; Unbreakable!; Unbeatable! –
How do you like me now?

They seethe because I dare to still breathe –
Like Through the eyes of a wise owl.
Imagine me wiping a lil' sweat from the ol' brow…
For heaven's sake – Not the God-Child!
Swiftly drifting through the throngs of an odd crowd.

Impenetrable; Un-breech-able;
By the Spirit of Truth – I just speak the unspeakable –
And preach the un-preach-able.

I'm too deep – They're still sleep.
I have a message for the wolf who likes to hunt and kill sheep:
I'm no innocent lamb chop – But I hop and will leap…
Over this hill's heap – And your deeds…You will reap!
Your seeds that you still keep – To fill creeks…
With most unfortunate and ill blossoms gives me the chills creep!
You're as the stench of a dead weed: Making daffodils weep.

I'm as the sweet fragrance of a rose – Inhaled through the nose,
Lungs, gills, and beaks.
     Notice the smeared streaks –
On my salt-stained and soft-teared cheeks.
     But I never cried; I leave you mystified by the gifts I hide –
As I *appear* weak.
     You slip and slide – Swinging fists of pride –
But within me – Inside? – No fear's piqued.
     I'm the unspoken question –
To the answer behind the headlights that the startled deer seeks.

     Who am I? – Master Unbreakable! That's who!
First name's Master!
     I hold the heat of the sun – That can dry up Alaska;
The heart of a glacier that can freeze out disaster!

     I can't be shut down! I won't be shut out!
That…hardly will be the case.
     I'm hard to be erased – Too far for you to chase;
Too strong for these iron bars I must embrace.
     Your hands are too small to hold the cards I had to face.
Sorry, Mr. Charlie, this car ain't got no brakes.
     Zoom! And I'm gone like a witch on her broom.
Bursting through the darkness and the gloom –
Like the head on a shroom.
     Life is such a bitch – I assume.
How did I get hitched to this doom?
     How did I get ditched?
Left like a carcass in a tomb?
     When the razors were pitched,
The blades' sharpness resumed.
     All that was well was consumed by hell –
Which were bricks in my concreted room.

Boom! I bloom out from under thick layers of dust –
From whence I rise.
My name gets caught in your throats –
As I lay hold of the bolts –
Of flashes of lightning that splashes the skies.
I've come from the ashes – Surprised?!
That I can't fold? That I won't mold or corrode?
Behold!
Here goes a hero with a story untold.

I've been to the worst parts:
Plotted on and cursed by perverse hearts.
I've been here before.
Like a repeated and raw form of rehearsed art.

And guess what?!
I'm UN-SHAKE-ABLE!
UNMISTAKEABLY UNBREAKABLE!
ALIVE and ENSATIABLE!
DRIVE…IRREPLACEABLE!
UN-BEAT-ABLE!
UNDEFEATABLE!
COURAGE SENSATIONAL!
Obstacles? Occasional.
But me…surrender easily as if breakable?
ABSOLUTELY INCAPABLE!

THE EVERLASTING; SHINING STAR

The world miscalculated cuz…
It thought it had the drop on him.
Mountains crush beneath his feet –
Because he walks on top of them.

Those below tried to talk him down:
He wouldn't hear of it.
They're miserable, disheartened, afraid,
And dispirited.

Since he learned he was a King,
His head's been – So above the clouds.
Casting not a single stare –
Upon the cares of the proud.

He has enemies pushing every button on his dial.
Blow! Open your eyes! Where are they now?

They say he's evil –
Cuz he speaks as if he is equal to a god.
And when he passes by, silence speaks the loudest –
So he only nods.

And every one of the odds stacked against him –
Is all vanity.
When he possesses heart and strength –
To lift up all humanity.

Cowards feign bravery – Pretending to be heroes.
Captured in self-slavery – Servants to their own, weak egos.

Not even knowing…that close by…the tornado twirls.
Blind! But keeping a close eye on the 'meat and potato' girls;

Going Nutts! While going for nuts –
Like elephants and squirrels.
    Yet, they quarrel with he who conquers self –
And conquers all the worlds.

    He overcomes –
They sink in the sands. But notice where he stands. –
    Atop the ocean –
With the entire land in both of his hands.

    Deep – In the creases of his palms –
They descend deeper and deeper.
    He who knows – And knows not that he knows –
Awake him! He is a sleeper!
    Nodding and drooling and drifting farther out of realities.
Illusionists! Fools! – With rudimentary mentalities.

    But they thought they had the drop on him.
Damn! Who miscalculated?
    The world! That's who!
Who underestimates and hates the self-elevated.

    The illuminated shines.
Wise and educated – He thinks!
    Enlightened mind of a scientist. –
From the pools of 'solutions', he drinks.

    Knowing the seven eyes of Truth –
That sees all and never blinks.
    But the dilated pupil of a lie? –
Behold how it winks.

    Emotions, with no control, are like guts sliced open:
They stink!
    Emotions – without a face – Is a mystery…
He's a sphinx.

Enigma!
Stigma on the flowers of immortality!
    If knowledge is food for thought,
Is not foolishness like daunted calories?

    The whole world is dreaming of some life –
While living a complete dream.
    Looking at everything that appears –
As only what it seems.

    They need a pattern; a group –
To be on somebody's team.
    But this one is strong!
Like black coffee with no sugar or cream.

    Alone – He and He who made him.
Stirred well and brewed to awake them –
    They can't break him – He must shake them!
Before their lower selves take them…

    To a place in the lower hells –
Where they can never be brought from.
    He ain't no 'Savior', 'Redeemer', or damn 'Messiah', -
Thought some.

    And so destruction caught 'em slippin' –
With no hunger to swallow pride.
    Who thought time would abide;
Now there's nowhere from truth they can hide.

    He's still marching and marching –
On that twelve step ladder he ascends.
    Climbing upward – Heaven-bound –
To where the temporary ends.

    The waters of the ocean are dried up –
Under the soul of his foot.

He avoids the worm –
Unlike the fish that's deceived by the hook.

That hook of awareness –
That reels in the end of man's fate.
Like the duck that quacks –
And then finds himself on the hunter's plate.

So the thunders can shake!
But still – No fear in him will they find.
The blind can't get near him.
Nor can they mirror in his climb.

Sublime; Supreme;
Gifted from the treasures of understanding.
Wisdom like high, octane jet fuel:
Flying: I don't think he's landing.

To think you had the drop on me –
Is like sinning in my garden.
But I walk in the cool with the fool –
With a heart unhardened.

Because my mood is not my final judgment.
Be grateful for that!
You can't take distastefulness, hatefulness,
And ungratefulness back.

But I can give you love instead –
And knowledge of who you are.
To the world, I am the sun:
The Everlasting Shining Star!

MORE THAN ONCE

Through the grief; Through the gloom –
When times were groggy; Through the grunts:
    You rushed to my side; swam through the tide –
Cried but you tried –
More than once.

    Under the clouds you were there –
Whether with wisdom or prayer –
    What could compare –
To the joy you brought?

    When trapped in life's winds –
And when the storm had me caught;
    In my weakest and most vulnerable state –
It was you who fought – More than once.

    When trials tested me…
Truly, it was the best for me.
    Impressively…you stood next to me –
In every word, deed, and thought.
    With strength most amazing,
You fought and you fought –
    I witnessed you battle all the giants that sought…
To separate, destruct, and destroy our alliance.
    You mastered the art of victory;
Broke 'conquering' down to a science.
    You dealt with me on the highest level
Of patience and compliance.
    Twas the prescription and medication
For my stubbornness and defiance.

    You became who I'd like to become:
Never hiding behind false fronts.

In your presence I find myself higher
Than the effects of a thousand and one blunts.
    You possess the love –
That every unloved and broken heart hunts.
    Frozen tears from my cold, brown eyes –
Betrayal ripped them away in chunks!
    But one thing is for certain: God don't make no junk!
At least that's the way you've made me feel – More than once.

    No matter the grief, disbelief –
Or the temporary beef that sidetracked us,
    You sustained and remained to be the water in my desert.
Otherwise, I'd have been one, fried cactus.

    The sword of adversity pierced,
Punctured, and penetrated, my feeble flesh.
    I was entangled in disparity;
In a web of unhappiness and misfortune's mesh.
    Around the difficulties and the stress;
The obstacles and the mess,
    I survived the kicks and the punts
Under strain and duress.

    Past all contests and all conquests…
You supported me…More than once.

    Your love helped me surpass all boundaries –
And break all barriers.
    I've been ill – Death has stood on my doorstep.
But what could be more scarier?
    …Than me losing you? Us not having each other?
When we have the tightest bond between man and woman –
Since, 'sister and brother'.

    Troubles and heartaches; Temptations and heart-breaks –
How much more can this weary heart take?

When I think of where I'd be without you…
This dreary heart shakes.
    Trembling;
Tremoring like the earth when it quakes.
    Before I deny that we go together –
Like Frosty and snowflakes.
    I would try taking a warm bath in ten, frozen lakes.
(And you know that's not possible!)

    Is the question, 'Do I love you?'
Are ten, naked women one problem for five monks?
    Okay then – Let me thank you more than once –
For not asking me that question again.

YOU KNOW WHAT I DID?

You know what I did this morning? I thought about you.
And I'll be damned! If those thoughts weren't sweeter –
Than the syrup I poured all over my pancakes!
I bet you'd taste better than that rye toast –
And those bran flakes that I poured inside of my bowl.
Before I'm lowered inside of that hole…
I gotta come forward with this side of my soul:
This side that is lonely…
Only because you're not lying on top of me –
Or at least…Right behind me.

You know what I did after you left?
I punched a hole in the wall with my left.
Then I held my breath through all the pain.
Not the pain in my hand…But the pain in my heart –
The pain would not subside;
It seemed that I would not survive.
I could have died.

But something that had been in me was gone forever!
I had been wrong to never-
Value your presence.
Especially after being captured by your original essence.

You know what I did? After it was all over?
My heart was cold as ice and hard all over.
I felt wounded and scarred all over.
It was all over –YOU!

You know what I did? Once it was all finished?
I tried to forget it ever started.
I don't understand.- How could a man?

So strong?
Be so weak and broken hearted?
    The moment you departed-
I was so dispirited; So disenchanted; So disoriented.
    Before we instated – our agreement to love and agree with
one another, I never knew you.
    It was better than first knowing you-
Then not knowing you anymore.
    What?-
Don't you know me anymore?

    You know what I did? Before I went to sleep last night?
I prayed that God would take away my memory of our last- night.
    The last time – My eyes embraced you –
My vision encased your delicacy;
    Other men were jealous of me.
And now I can't think about no one else.
It's almost like celibacy.

    You know what I did? When I played our favorite song?
What else? I played our favorite song again and again.
    So far gone…So deep down.
I just wanted to be through with it.
    Instead, I found myself dialing your number-
But I couldn't go through with it.
    I may have done it to myself –
But I swore to myself that you did it.
    I stuck on you like whatever you gave me –
Brought about all that.
    Yet, when I had it, I didn't know what to do with it!
What do I do? Now? I'm still wondering.

    You know what I did? After I thought about all this?
I reminisced.
    On how many times you and I fought about all this.

I reflected on the good times.
    As well as the bad times –
That were brought about because of all this.
    Because of all this –
I was willing to risk all this!
    At the time, I told myself , 'No sense in trying to fake all this.'
    When I know damn well –
I can't take all this.
    And now I sit here and miss all of that…
That's the honest truth.

    You know what I did? After I wrote this all down?
I realized how I somehow turned all smiles into all frowns.
    Men!-

I ask myself sometimes, 'Are we all clowns?'
    I'll be the first to admit.
That it's all ego that makes us all fall down.
    But look out for me!
Because I'm getting back up again!

    You know what I did? To make myself feel better?
I decided to sit down and write you this letter.
    And I hope it reaches you in time.
Because being without you-
Should be a serious crime.
    Every relationship blossoms to maturity –
But each in its time.
    Even after it reaches its prime-
It's still not perfect.
    I want you back!
But I want you to know – That I'm still not perfect.

    I don't know what I'd do –
If you didn't want me anymore;

If you didn't need me anymore;
If you didn't miss me anymore;
If you didn't want to kiss me anymore;
if you didn't want to hug me anymore;
If you didn't love me anymore –
I just don't know what I'd do.

Because you know what I did –
I messed up bad!
And if you want to know -
What I'm going to do to keep you.
After I get you back –
I'll show you.
But first…You have to decide what you want to do.
I already told you what I'd do.

I NEED YOU!

There's something I need to say;
Something I need to express.
I need to confess!
And allow my needs to be addressed.
I need you in my life and I need to be in yours.
I need you today - But tomorrow, I'll need you even more!
More than ever before –
I need you more than just a little while.
I need the way you excite me -
With more than just a little smile.
I need your love: Innocent like and adorable, little child.
I needed you from the beginning .
This need is more than just a little now.
This heart in me –
Needs you to be a part of me.
The harder we – Strive; The farther we – Drive:
Just like it ought to be.
It's hard for me.
I didn't always have my father to father me.
And it bothered me –
That my mother and I weren't that camaraderie.
These veins bleed pain –
The pain that tears through every artery.
I need you to help me rise –
When my eyes start to get watery.
I need you with all my might –
I need you for your strength.
I need you with all my sight.
I need you to help me go the length –
I need you to be the 'I' in my sight.
I need you to be my engine and my wings.

When it's going to be a flight;
Not just in my corner but in the ring –
When it's going to be a fight.
I need you to be on my left –
I need you to be on my right -
In the darkest night,
I need you to be my brightest light.
I need you to understand how much I need you to need me.
I locked myself inside of my own dark world –
And Baby?
It was your love that freed me!
And I'll say it again if need be –
Him need she –
Her need him…
However it goes…We need 'WE'!
Lord , I need her to push me –
I dream of the day she puts me…
Deep in her mushy cookie;
Bathing in her gushy nooky.
Awe , sookie-sookie! –
Look where she done took me-
Father forgive me –
But I think she done hooked me!
And if needing her is sin –
Then hell's gonna cook me.
If loving her's a crime –
They should've already booked me!
I need you with the worst of me –
To love the very best of me.
I need you to thirst for me –
From one part of me to the rest of me.
I need you to be the air in my lungs.
When I feel like I'm going to drown.
I need you to be my umbrella when the rain comes down –
And keeps coming down.

I need you to be the melody in my music;
The lyrics to my song.
I need you to be strong –
Without asking , "For what?" or, "How long?"
I need you to close your eyes –
And imagine I'm the only one near.
Because baby , I just opened my eyes and realized –
You're the only one here.
I need you to be my rope and my saddle.
When climbing the slopes in life's travels.
When I can't cope and can't straddle;
When life says, "Nope," And snakes rattle.
I need you to have my back –
Like my coat and my shadow.
When storms leave me fragile; -
Broken and soaked on grief's gravel.
I need you to be my boat and my paddles;
My forbidden apple –
And hope in all my battles.
I need you to believe me when I tell you ,"I need you!"
Because I wouldn't have said it if I never felt the need to.

LET ME...

Let me show you a life that you've never had;
Make up for every good day that somehow just turned bad.
I'm going CRAZY over you –
Because I'm so CRAZY about you!
Let me tell you why I don't want to spend
Another waking moment without you.
Let me show you how much I adore you.
Let me give you the attention you deserve.
I'm attracted beyond comprehension –
To every dimension - Of your every curve.

You stir something up inside of me.
And it's earth shaking and ground-breaking.
Let me show you this picture I have –
Of us constantly and constantly love-making.
There's no faking; I'm anxious and aching.
To feel the heat of your tongue.
Let me show you how to breathe deeper -
Breathe Baby!
Breathe deep from your lungs.

Let me show you true passion:
Sincere, genuine, and honest.
I swear I won't leave you broken; broken hearted;
I won't break one promise.
Let me treat you like a Queen;
Vibrate your palace like thunder can.
You're body's my castle –
Let me fall in your hole like Alice in Wonderland .

Don't be afraid to love me.
Be brave and swallow you tears.

When sorrow appears…take me inside of your heart.
And let me bottle your tears.
    I pray that tomorrow is near –
Because I can't wait to spend another day with you!
    I can't wait until the night -
The moon shines on our nakedness –
As I lay with you!

    Sweaty and wet –
But let me see how wet I can make it.
    Let me see how long I can go on before –
You just can't take it.
    Let me show you why I'm so different –
From every other guy – In your life.
    Because I'm a man –
And that boy? –
Just didn't know what to do with a wife.
    Let me rest your legs on the planets.
And show you the stars while I explore you tropical worlds.
    I would have been proud to father ten of your children.
Even if they all were unstoppable girls.

    Let me be your buddy and companion.
Let me show you a friendship that truly can exist.
    Let me show you that it feels so good –
And Baby, it won't ever again…
Get as good as this!
    You know why you fell in love with me –
Almost the very moment you met me?
    Cuz I can touch you, kiss you, lick you.
And love you the right way.
All you have to do is just let me.

THE BEACH AND THE SAND

I saw the beach slowly rising.
Tricklets of cool water from a bitter ocean –
Painted my face blue.
   As the powerful and mighty waves
Brushed against the shores,
Bright skies stared down – Smiling at me.
   Waving clouds –
Traveled across to their unexplored destinations.
Empty?
   The wind cried – With each whistling breeze;
As if saddened by something unknown.

   I saw the beach…
And the sand – Rapidly lifting – Higher and higher.
   Teardrops from the sun frowning.
Then something truly amazed me: Teardrops of fire!
…Descended upon my immediate parameters.
Life on earth's navigated by its rays.
   Sorrow form the sun rained down vehemently –
Melting the very ground where which I stood.
Entranced and in awe!
What is the meaning of this vision?

   I saw the beach and the sand…
Hastily ascending.
Breathless was I – And paralyzed from a distance.
   I stand here;
   Here stands I –
   And here I stand.
But here is so far away; There is too close.
   Gathering birds –
Chirping; Unaware of my ability to exist.

Swans with wings – Stretched out -Yearning to assist.
Lamenting! In the skies directly above me.
What am I saying?
The scent of ocean life is slowly…
Fading. And fading. And fading.
All immobile; No hint of motion of life.
The days are getting sleepy.
The nights have been so creepy.

I saw the beach and the sand…
Now mounting the horizons.
Heaven is running away.
Pursue it I must.
Pursue it - I can't.
Deception's beyond the blue.
The trees seem to panic and quiver with guilt;
As they withhold their branches and conceal their budding.
The four corners of the earth close in – All around me…
As if to conceal nature – In her flawless beauty.
Flawless and unblemished nudity.

Life is changing colors with each vanishing second.
The Son maintains his position and point of view.
But the sky isn't waving back –While shading black
And fading away.
In front of me lies a broken hour-glass.
Time no longer remembers my name.
Time tells the truth. But the clock is the liar.
This is mystery.
I saw the beach and the sand…
Elevating expeditiously.
But somehow – The beach has never risen from its nesting.
Thoughts of moments missed.
Advantages lost.
Opportunities stolen.

Rush upon me!
Like ants to a honey farm – Or a lover's picnic.
   My feet betray me.
Why is it so cold under the sun?
Frigid.
   Defiant are the legs which walked away with my hope
And betrayed my faith for a lofty price.
   Sand inhabits the crevices of my nostrils.
Down must be the way to the other side:
To the better side.
   Is it better?
So many memories unfold. So I can't see them.

   To remember the last time – I've tasted oxygen?
I just can't remember.
   The morning mourns.
And somehow…I was cheated out of my warnings.
I cheated for it all.
I was cheated out of it all.
   So much left to say;
So much left to do.
   O' beach!
How heavy is the weight of it?
   This is it!
I can no longer stand.
I can no longer feel the ground under me.
I can no longer feel the ground above me.
   On top of me!
My vision is no more –
Such as my life from the beginning.
Now I get it!
   Now I look.
I look at now.
Where am I? I am here?

In the belly of the quicksand –
Which swallowed me like a cold beverage.

It all happened so quick.
Life O' Life!
But a glimpse and a glare.
No signs of struggles –
As my tears solidify into grains -
Of brown, dirty, gritty specks.
That's it!
Now I get it again! For real this time!
This unfamiliar land upon which I stand…
My life from the beginning – Which had no beginning…
I've been sinking in the sand.

FROM ME TO YOU

If I had a brush – I would paint you 'Beautiful'!
No matter the dark colors or shades you're going through.
Am I boring you?
I hope not. Cuz you mean the world to me!
When you got down; Didn't turn back around –
I knew God found my girl for me.
You're my star and my light –
No matter how black or dead my sky.
I'ma fight to make it back to you –
Even if they black my eye.

If I was a spoon –
I'd stir inside of your sweetness.
You're the fruit of my desire.
I think I'll call you Peaches.

If I had your lips and your tongue –
I'd probably leave you speechless.
I'm struggling without you –
Trying to overcome and come over this weakness.

If I had to get arrested –
Why couldn't I be captured and detained by your body-talk?
Handcuffed by the seductive sway in your hips?
I think it's…It's got to be that naughty walk.

I may sound silly.
(But you know…) I'm just thinking right now.
Where is everybody?
What? Am I stinking right now?
I'm trying to be a BIGGER man –
And keep from shrinking right now.

Instead of rocking your boat, I was abandoning ship –
And that's probably why I'm sinking right now.

But if I had a lifejacket,
I'd swim through your wet sea…
To a shore far away –
Where it's just you and me.

And if I had a pencil –
I would put all this on paper.
Although thoughts kept in the heart –
Are thoughts better kept safer.
You've gotta be in the safety of my heart.
Because you're a thought of mine every, single day.
And if I had my way –
I would never stop loving me. Would you?

WILL YOU TRUST ME?

Will you trust me to love you like you love me? Will you trust me again and tell me you still love me? Even though I've been careless in the past with your love and trust?

You gave me the gift of your heart and mind; every inch; every element; every part. Will you trust me not to use and abuse those gifts again? Will you trust me to travel the distance from your brain to your heart, which seems like eighteen eternities but is only eighteen inches apart?

Will you trust me to open my eyes and notice your tears: The ones I was once blind to due to my selfish and self-centered ways? Will you trust me to listen when you need someone to talk to? Will you trust me to become more open to your ideas and suggestions?

Will you trust me to be more romantic and less barbaric? Telling you how beautiful, attractive, and desirable you really are? Being more complimentary and less argumentative? Will you trust me to be more understanding: Controlling my aggressions and emotions at those times when you or I find myself trying to control the woman in her emotional state?

Will you trust me to bring you joy and make you happy in your periods of sadness? Will you trust me to be the one to never make the other one cry? Will you trust me to be able to make you smile no matter how hard I cry? Will you forgive me for all those times I made you frown?

Will you trust me to be more caring, compassionate, and sensitive? To your concerns, pain, and painful concerns? Will you trust me to be more sympathetic to your feelings?

Will you trust me to be more compassionate about your passions? Will you trust me to be more thoughtful and respectful to who you are, what you mean, and what you *should* mean to me as my woman, my help, and my blessing?

Will you trust me to trust your instincts and intuitions? Will you trust me to be more considerate towards your femininity?

Will you trust me with your secrets, embarrassments, and discretions? Will you trust me not to mishandle your desires and not to ignore or neglect your simplest requests? Will you trust me to be more embracing and accepting to the love for me that lies deep within the woman who is inside of you? Will you trust me to introduce satisfaction to your disoriented and discontented heart?

Will you trust me to feed your sexual cravings from the spoons of pleasure? Will you trust me to be only attracted and completely faithful to you and only you? Will you trust me to touch you and kiss you in places where ecstasy is aroused?

Will you trust me to be careful and delicate with your heart, mind, body, and soul? Will you trust me to treat you like a woman should be treated by her man? With no explanations or excuses?

Will you trust me to be reliable? Someone you can depend on? Will you trust me to be strong where I used to be weak? Will you trust me to be your friend and confidante? Will you trust me to be someone you can turn to instead of someone who will turn on you? Will you trust me to be a shoulder you can always lean on?

Will you trust me to walk with you? Never run away when things don't run our way? *Always* lie *next* to you and *never* lie *to* you? Will you trust me inside of your, mind, heart, and body? Will you trust me to say what I mean and mean everything I say to you? Will you trust me to always tell the honest truth to you and trust the fact and truth that we belong together; that we are were made for each other and that's the honest truth?

Will you trust me to walk with you? To never run away or walk out of your life? Will you trust me with the keys to your heart again?

Can you trust me again?

Will you trust me to change and make it different from before? Will you trust me to adore you even more?

Will you trust yourself to let go of the past and just love me now and forevermore? Will you trust me? I just want to know.

GOOD...WILL YOU COME BACK TO ME?

I care when no one cares for me –
Aware of everyone who stares at me.
"Look – He's got his own mind;
"He plants his seeds, grows his fruits,
"And plucks from his own vine!
"He's in his own thoughts; in his own moment.
"And in his own time.
"He's his own person; takes his own position –
"That's a stone crime!"

"Now…let us praise him –
With the highest form negativity –
Which is the highest energy and praise"
I find ways to find ways.
And you can't help but to admire me in my ways.

Good…will you come back to me?
That, might I ask before it's too late?
Before the storm of my rage –
Engages with destiny to brew fate?
Help me now hate all that I love –
And now love all that makes me stew hate.
Born in the state of unknowing:
Son growing in God- state.
And if God states:
That which I declare why would Heaven wait?
I am here. So I am there.
I am the scale and the weight.

Good…will you come back to me?
I already know you will.

I am the wheel balance in the universe.
I'm so everywhere, I appear still.
    I'm the heavenly dew on the grass;
At the bottom of the mountains – chilled.
    I'm the fresh blanket of snow –
That highlights the tops of the hills.
    I'm the spring of the water; the salt of the sea.
The skies remember me well.
    They can testify that I was an angel in flight –
Until something decided to bring me to hell.

    Good…Will you come back to me? No, I can't ask.
I smile from time to time. Each smile's a different mask though.
    To be relaxed; to be healed; to know that 'peace' is slippery –
Patience is a unique power – With it comes epiphany.

    I've got to be out of my mind –
To fraternize with similar conditions as these.
    I've got to be out of my body –
To weather myself to better positions – I squeeze –
    This emptiness with the grips of my emotions –
Letting go of what's got a hold on me.
    When the roads were as smooth as lotion –
And I didn't have this load on me.
    If only, 'if', can save me now –
After my most trusted have rolled on me…
    A baby can see what eighty year olds can't see:
Innocence!

    Good…Will you come back to me?
Never mind I asked.
    Because I applaud this stage:
The actors and the supporting cast.
    To be seen; to be heard about – I'm not concerned about.
To be yearned; to be learned – Isn't that what everyone chases?

To be burned by evil smiles on loving faces:
Such an ugly basis.
    To be forgiving;
To forget what the world couldn't do for me?
That's what everyone thinks.
    The wave was good –
But when the wave is no more…
Doesn't everyone sink?
    The water's heavy when the good is gone.
What is formed by the pressure on a cornerstone?
(Is it not a diamond?)

    To be noticed for all that is against good?
Where is the glory?
    To be the center of attraction? Unhealthy interactions?
Not my story…(No more that is).
    On the verge of breathing fire –
Through icy, cold barrels –
    No thought for the eye;
No regard for the sparrow.
    The chances of 'good' –
Coming back to me are slim and narrow.
    But I arrow no one with the same envy
Everyone arrows at me.

STILL DADDY'S

Still Daddy's lil' girl; still Daddy's lil' Lady;
No matter how many birthdays: Still Daddy's lil' Baby!

Yesterday, you were my everything; today, you still are.
Tomorrow, you'll still be – Daddy's lil' star.

You're still Daddy's!

Still my chocolate diamond; pink ruby –
Still my heart's crystal and pearl;
Still my gorgeous lil' Princess;
Still Daddy's lil' girl.

Still the wind in my breath;
Still all that I have when there's nothing left;
Still my MVP no matter the refs;
I'm still your shelter, cape; your rock in your cleft.

Still Daddy's!

Today's your special day and tomorrow still will be.
You can ask me for the world – And that's for real –
So feel free,
Because time is moving fast as time slowly drifts.
I'm still yours; you're still Daddy's – With or without the gifts.

You still mean everything to my heart.
It still hurts when we're apart.
I still love you as much as I did –
From the start of the very start.

You're still my future; You're still my tomorrow –
You're still part of a good life I enjoyed.

You're still Daddy's lil' Soul-Day girl.
That's still a part you can't avoid.
And the truth that can never be destroyed.

Still Daddy's!

BABY BOY

You mean everything to my heart.
It hurts that we're apart.
I can see you now growing –
So handsome and smart.

Daddy owes you the world; to shower you with gifts.
I'm missing you so much as time slowly drifts.

My future; my tomorrow;
My minute by minute joy.
Past, present, future, or eternity:
You'll always be Daddy's baby boy!

THIS IS WHAT BIRTHDAYS ARE FOR

For me to write you poetry –
Hey aren't you impressed?
Aren't birthdays for me to tell you,
"I love you and wish you the best?"
…For me to tell you just - How great you are in my eyes?
For me to jump out of the dark and start yelling, "Surprise!"
For me to say, "Happy Birthday," –
And wish you plenty more?
Truly, this is what birthdays are truly for.

Laughter and excitement ; smiles pasted on our faces.
Unwrapping all the gifts; taking trips to the wildest places.
Weekend-filled celebration and parties galore!
D.J.'s playing our favorite songs –
This is what birthdays are for!

To never forget - But to always remember.
To share intimate moments with loved ones and family members.
To be with the ones you care about;
With whom you make that perfect connection;
To smother you with immeasurable love!
And shower you with uncontrollable affection.
To show you how in our hearts,
We hold you near and dear;
To tell you we love you just as much –
Every day of the year;
To wish you all the joy life could have in store – Truly…
This is what birthdays are for!

WONDERING

I'm wondering where you are –
I'm wondering what you are doing.
I'm wondering where we've come thus far –
Considering the chemistry we have brewing.
I'm wondering if you are wondering about me –
And why I'm wondering about you so much.
I'm wondering if this means anything to you.
I'm wondering if you'll keep in touch.

IT ALL COMES WITH BEING A MOTHER

She delivered a child – Love unconditional –
In her heart she vowed.
Whether she cried or smiled; bent over backwards
Or bowed:
All of it came with being a mother.

The risks she would take; the rules she would break;
The obstacles that were at stake.
The dinners she would make;
Birthday cakes she would bake –
All of it came with being a mother.

From tummy-aches and flus –
To new shoes and school clothes –
Coming home from the playground –
With black eyes and a bruised nose.
In the midst of the storms; beyond the clouds –
Who can mistake her?
Whether you're Mommy's little Angel –
Or Mommy's little trouble maker…
It all came with being your mother.

She's somewhere close at all times.
She's always easy to be found.
Although she knows she can't and won't –
Always be around.
Many nights, by her,
You were bathed and tucked under the covers.
Through the years, she shed so many tears –
But it all comes with being a mother.

There was dirt and muddy tracks.
She came a long way and many miles were covered.
The belt made some, 'smacks'.
But with her kisses and smiles –
Her child was smothered.
Because all of it comes with being a mother.

Good, bad, ups, and downs –
It's all made to fit together.
Somehow, she was always ready and prepared –
To wrestle the winds of bad weather.
Disappointments overwhelmed her at one time or another.
But all of this and more is what came with being a mother.

Sometimes it felt so good;
Sometimes it felt so bad.
Sometimes Mama seemed so glad –
Sometimes she seemed more sad.
Some days she was tired and wearied with
This, that or the other.
But no matter what – Who doesn't love her?
Because that's what comes with being a mother.

YOU ARE MY BLESSING!

It was long nights of turmoil – Hardly ever resting.
First, it was bitterness, rage, and revenge deeply infesting…
(All inside of me).

All seemed dark, gone, lost, or dead – Couldn't figure out
why life was depriving me.

Tell me with your lips…
Why your lips alone seem to be reviving me.

Don't look down now.
But there appears to be an up-rise in me.

Mmmm, mmm, mmm, I heard you laugh last night.
And I could've sworn I hear the Angels playing my song.

Then I heard your serious tone –
And realized you were meant for me all along.

Baby, you are my blessing!
Can't wait to get to the kisses, hugging, and caressing.

What?
Well, ain't no sense in suppressing.

What I'm feeling about knocking that down;
Dipping my biscuits in your gravy –
And sopping that down.

Now ain't no stopping, rehearsing,
Or turning around.

I'm up in here like,
"Naa, na, na, naa, na! Look what I found!"

You are my blessing!
This might be better than a plate –
Of my Mama's turkey and dressing.

I prayed for you.
And you're even more than I dreamed.

I was losing the game.
You looked past that, suited up and hopped on my team.

You're like a drug and I'm a fiend…
Fiending for your hot mocha, brown sugar…
Mo' cream.
	I was looking for that fa' sho' thing:
That now that I got you, 'I can't let choo go thing'
	Forget trying to figure out what it is
Or what it means.
	I believe that what we've found –
Are the lyrics to our own love theme.
	You are my blessing!
Pulling on the strings of my affection;
	A gift to the man I am –
And his every expression.
	In our far separation –
There's this close connection.
	I just can't deny it.
I want to stick you and give you this injection.
	I love your complexion!
And how when I look in your eyes…
I see my reflection.
	You're perfect for me if for no one else.
You don't need no correction.
	I'ma vote for you to be the Queen of my heart –
Until you win the election.
	Because after complete inspection –
There's no other selection.
Cuz Baby, you are my blessing!

CPSIA information can be obtained
at www.ICGtesting.com
Printed in the USA
FSOW02n1617220515
7356FS

9 781481 765794